The Lodekka Alternatives

The Lodekka Alternatives

STEWART J. BROWN

Ian Allan
PUBLISHING

First published 2013

ISBN 978 0 7110 3535 5

© Ian Allan Publishing Ltd 2013

Published by Ian Allan Publishing Ltd, Hersham, Surrey KT12 4RG.

Printed in England.

Visit the Ian Allan Publishing website at www.ianallanpublishing.com

Copyright

Picture Credits

COVER: Three of the models which copied the layout of the Lodekka with an Aldershot & District Dennis Loline (top), a Central SMT Albion Lowlander (bottom left) and a City of Oxford AEC Renown (bottom right). John May, Harry Hay, Geoffrey Morant

PAGE 1: The first and last batches of Dennis Lolines for Aldershot & District are represented in this view. Nearer the camera is a 1965 Mk III with Weymann body, while alongside is an original 1958 model with East Lancs body. They carry Aldershot & District rather than Dennis badges underneath the radiator filler cap. With 141 in its fleet, Aldershot & District was the biggest Loline operator. John May

PAGE 2: Full-fronted low-height buses were rare. The only Lowlanders to feature full-width fronts were those supplied to Ribble. Alexander built the bodies. This bus is seen in Wigan in 1974, freshly repainted in NBC's corporate poppy red. Stewart J. Brown

ABOVE: The two Leyland Lowloader prototypes were purchased by Lowland Motorways of Glasgow in the spring of 1957. This was the older of the two, with a Saunders Roe body. The full-width front with deep windscreens made it look like a trolleybus. There was no external access to the cab on either of the Lowloaders; the driver entered from the passenger saloon by a door in the front bulkhead. Both buses were sold by Lowland at the end of 1957. Geoffrey Morant

CONTENTS

INTRODUCTION

Inspired by the Bristol Lodekka, each of Britain's main bus chassis manufacturers developed low-height models in the 1950s and 1960s – double-deck buses with a centre gangway on both decks and a nominal overall height of 13ft 6in rather than the standard 14ft 6in. Leyland's original rear-engined Lowloader did not get beyond the prototype stage but was the genesis of the successful Atlantean. AEC's Bridgemaster of 1956 was of conventional layout but unconventional integral construction, marrying AEC's resources with those of Crossley and Park Royal, sister companies within the Associated Commercial Vehicles group. The pre-production Crossley-developed Bridgemasters were attractive buses, the square top-heavy-looking Park Royal production buses less so. Dennis built Lodekkas under licence from 1957, with varying degrees of success; half of all Loline sales went to one operator.

Next, in 1959, came Guy with the Wulfrunian, a bus ahead of its time – and a major failure, one operator taking 90% of production, and most vehicles being withdrawn on the expiry of their original seven-year Certificates of Fitness rather than being recertified for further service as was the norm for heavy-duty buses of the time. Not within the scope of this volume, which looks at relatively short-lived models which sold in limited numbers, was the next low-height model, Daimler's phenomenally successful Fleetline, launched in 1960.

Then came Leyland, in 1961, with the Albion Lowlander, developed to address the Scottish Bus Group's requirement for a low-height version of the Titan PD3. SBG accounted for 70% of Lowlander sales. The last low-height model to be launched, in 1962, was the AEC Renown, a bus which, we can say with hindsight, was behind its time in a world where the Atlantean and the Fleetline represented the future.

Between them, these models effectively killed the side-gangway lowbridge bus. After the last big deliveries of lowbridge PD3s to SBG companies in 1961, very few lowbridge buses were built – just 20 between 1962 and 1967, when the last was delivered to Bedwas & Machen Urban District Council in South Wales.

None of the low-height models was a great success. Sales of the four conventional models, Bridgemaster, Loline, Lowlander and Renown, totalled fewer than 700 over 12 years, an average of fewer than 60 a year, shared by three manufacturers – AEC, Dennis and Leyland. That compares with deliveries of production Lodekkas averaging almost 350 a year.

So what can be seen as Lodekka look-alikes failed to emulate the success of the original, of which 5,217 were produced from the appearance in service of the first prototype in 1949 to the final FLFs in 1968. But they did make an interesting diversion from the more popular mainstream models.

My thanks to those who helped in the preparation of this book. Mike Eyre worked his magic on most of the illustrations, and provided all of those which are credited to John May, Roy Marshall, Geoffrey Morant, Arnold Richardson and Peter Roberts. Thanks too, to Richard Morant. The Omnibus Society library was a useful source of reference, and the work done by the PSV Circle and its members over the last 70 years has created an archive which is invaluable to all transport authors.

Stewart J. Brown
Hebden Bridge
July 2013

Chapter One

AN ENGINEERING CHALLENGE

ABOVE: The first successful low double-decker was developed at the end of the 1920s, with the fitting of side-gangway lowbridge bodywork to a new generation of low-framed chassis, led by the Leyland Titan and the AEC Regent. The lowbridge body reduced the overall height of the bus from around 14ft 6in to around 13ft 6in. This is a Leyland Titan TD2 with 48-seat lowbridge Leyland body, delivered to Alexander's of Falkirk in 1932 and operated until 1950. Leyland

ABOVE: Bristol and Eastern Coach Works produced two prototypes of what would become the hugely successful Lodekka. This is the first, photographed in 1949 before delivery to the grandly titled Bristol Tramways & Carriage Company. The chassis design allowed a centre gangway on both decks within a body that was 13ft 6in high. Both prototypes had exposed radiators, unlike production models, which had new-look fronts. ECW

It's difficult to overstate the importance of the Leyland Titan TD1. It brought together in 1927 all the features of what would for the next 30-odd years count as a modern double-deck bus. The driver was located right at the front of the chassis, alongside the engine, still petrol when the TD1 was introduced. And the chassis frame was lower than on most previous designs, having been purpose-built for bus operation rather than adapted from a lorry chassis.

With a central gangway on both decks the Titan was 14ft 6in high. But by locating the upper-deck gangway on the offside of the body, then lowering it by one foot, its height could be reduced to just 13ft 6in – handy in areas with low railway bridges, in a country which still had an extensive railway network.

There were two drawbacks with what was known as the lowbridge body. Passengers sitting on the offside of the lower saloon had to be careful not to bang their heads on the intrusion created by the sunken gangway; a warning to this effect was usually displayed on the backs of the lower-deck seats. And on the upper deck the side gangway meant that the standard seating layout comprised rows of four-passenger benches with limited headroom. So if, on a fully loaded bus, you were sitting on the nearside of the upper saloon you had not only to bend double to get out but also to squeeze past three other people.

Conductors had mixed views of lowbridge buses. Some liked the convenience of being able to balance themselves with their backs against the

offside of the body on the top deck, and not having to turn from side to side to collect fares. Others disliked having to stretch to collect fares from passengers sitting on the nearside. Generally, the view amongst operators, passengers and probably most conductors was that the centre-gangway highbridge bus was a more spacious and better-designed vehicle.

The first serious challenge to the lowbridge double-decker came from Bristol, which in 1949 built the first of two prototypes of what would become the Lodekka. This had a drop-centre rear axle and had the propeller shaft offset from the centre line of the chassis, allowing the lower-saloon gangway to be lower than on a conventional chassis. A second prototype, in 1950, had a differential behind the gearbox and two propshafts. Both buses were bodied by Eastern Coach Works, entering service with Bristol Tramways and West Yorkshire Road Car respectively. The drivetrain layout meant that the Lodekka had centre gangways on both decks, but within an overall height of 13ft 6in.

Sales of the Lodekka were restricted to state-owned companies, and the model was the standard – indeed, from 1958 the only – choice for the British Transport Commission's bus companies buying double-deckers in England and Wales. The only other buyers of the Lodekka were subsidiaries of the Scottish Bus Group. However, other operators were keen to take advantage of this new approach to bus design, and the leading builders of double-deck bus chassis were eager to meet their needs.

Leyland was first, and with a radical approach. One of the obstacles faced in producing a low-height bus was the propeller shaft running from the engine at the front to the axle at the rear. Leyland's answer was to relocate the engine, mounting it at the back of the bus. For its Lowloader Leyland used a more compact engine than was fitted to the contemporary Titan PD2, fitting the 5.76-litre O.350 in place of the latter's 9.8-litre O.600. Two prototypes were built, the first in 1952 with a full-front Saunders-Roe body which made it look like a trolleybus without booms, the second in 1954, with a half-cab body by Metro-Cammell. These were both 27ft-long rear-entrance buses and had the front axle located in the normal position, under the driver's cab. When the legal length limit was increased to 30ft in 1956 Leyland was ready with an even more radical rear-engined design which took advantage of the new legislation and had the front axle set back to allow an entrance opposite the driver, and which was powered by an O.600 engine. Thus was born what would become the Atlantean, although

LEFT: The Bristol Lodekka was the definitive low-height bus, initially as the LD model, with rear-entrance ECW body normally seating 60. This Eastern Counties bus, new in 1957, was an LD5G, with Gardner 5LW engine.
Stewart J. Brown

by the time it entered production in 1958 it was no longer a low-height vehicle.

AEC, the other main builder of double-deckers in the 1950s, was next in the field, unveiling its Bridgemaster in 1956. Like Leyland, AEC took advantage of the new legislation on vehicle length, and the first Bridgemasters were 30ft long, although a short-wheelbase model (16ft 6in, rather than 18ft 10in) was available with an overall length of 27ft 8in. Unlike Leyland, AEC adopted a conventional mechanical layout retaining a front-mounted engine driving the rear axle. Where it did depart from convention was in its integral construction. AEC was part of the Associated Commercial Vehicles group, which owned Crossley, Park Royal and Roe. The first four pre-production vehicles were built by Crossley, and a fifth was completed by Harkness of Belfast using a structure supplied by Crossley. All of the production Bridgemasters which followed were built by Park Royal using an ungainly steel-framed body rather than the stylish aluminium-framed structure produced by Crossley. This was done to meet the needs of the British Electric Traction group, a significant customer for AEC.

The first two Bridgemasters were fitted with the 7.7-litre AV470 103bhp engine, a power unit deemed adequate for a bus conceived as a 27ft-long model, before the legislation was revised to allow 30ft buses; all subsequent Bridgemasters, irrespective of length, used the more powerful 125bhp 9.6-litre AV590. The engine was installed in a subframe, similar to that used on the Routemaster which was being developed for London Transport, and this

carried not just the engine but also the four-speed synchromesh gearbox, the independent coil-spring front suspension, the radiator and steering. The rear subframe had the rear suspension units – coil springs on early vehicles, but air suspension on most. Braking was by an unusual air-hydraulic system which featured air operation of an hydraulic master cylinder for the front brakes. This was necessary because there was insufficient space to fit air brake chambers on the front hubs. The rear brakes were air-operated.

The first two Bridgemasters, which were badged as Crossleys, entered service in 1956 after being exhibited at that year's Commercial Motor Show, where the magazine *Passenger Transport* described them 'as outstanding among the new

BELOW: The ingenious layout of the Leyland Lowloader prototypes can be seen in this view of the first of the two, with bodywork by Saunders Roe. The compact 0.350 engine is mounted in the rear offside corner, under the rearward-ascending staircase. The photograph shows the absence of a step between the gangway and the lower saloon, which in turn reduced the overall height of the bus. Note also the engine access doors and the radiator filler located alongside the rear window.
British Commercial Vehicle Museum

ABOVE: The second of the Leyland Lowloader prototypes, seen in the ownership of Buckmaster of Leighton Buzzard, which operated it in the 1960s. It had a Metro-Cammell body with 61 seats. This bus still exists and is currently awaiting restoration. Geoffrey Morant

models introduced by ACV Sales' – which, if you think about it, is a rather limited complement. Vehicle 001 (which had been inside Earl's Court) was an MB3RA model with the standard manual gearbox and was delivered to Walsall Corporation. Vehicle 002 (which had been in the demonstration park) was registered 9 JML and after some general demonstration work was loaned in 1957 to Birmingham City Transport, by which it was later purchased. It was the last front-engined bus to join the Birmingham fleet, and although a non-standard type in a highly standardised fleet it was operated for 12 years. The two AV470-engined Bridgemasters incorporated a transfer box for the offset driveline on which the propeller shaft was located to the left of the vehicle. This was not needed on the AV590-powered buses, on which the engine and gearbox were angled slightly. Demonstrator 002 was the only Bridgemaster to have a semi-automatic gearbox and was thus an MB2RA model; all other vehicles had four-speed manual gearboxes.

Bridgemaster demonstrators 003 (60 MMD) and 004 (76 MME) took to the road in 1957 and were later purchased by South Wales Transport and Barton Transport respectively. And 005 was the

bus completed by Harkness, built for Belfast Corporation. It was the first new motor bus for Belfast since 1953 and was operated for 12 years. These three vehicles had the standard combination of AV590 engine and manual gearbox, and were thus B3RA models.

The next manufacturer to enter the fray was Dennis. The Guildford-based firm had built a small number of its Lance double-deck model in the years following World War 2 – a precise 100 between 1947 and 1954, of which 72 went to local BET subsidiary Aldershot & District. Dennis was not exactly a significant force in the bus business, nor did it have the engineering or financial resources of the industry giants, Leyland and AEC. So it took a short-cut, securing a licensing agreement with Bristol, which allowed it to build a chassis derived from the Lodekka. Indeed early advertising for the new model, named the Loline, featured a standard ECW-bodied Bristol LD with a photograph retouched to incorporate a Dennis grille. The original sales brochure noted: 'Due to the inverted arch construction of the rear axle and the offset transmission line the Loline chassis permits a conveniently low rear step with complete freedom of access to both saloons.'

The Loline was originally offered with the choice of Dennis's own 120bhp 8-litre engine or the 112bhp 8.4-litre Gardner 6LW, but in the event there were no Dennis-engined Lolines. Dennis also used its own five-speed manual gearbox and its own drop-centre rear axle which was 'built in the Dennis works by craftsmen', according to the company's brochure. The axle was derived from that used on the Lodekka. A significant advance over the Lodekka was the use of air brakes, with wider front brake shoes. A prototype chassis was exhibited at the 1956 Commercial Motor Show but was never bodied. The Loline was designed for 30ft long bodywork and had an 18ft 6in wheelbase.

Dennis had to find a bodybuilder, as sales of ECW bodies, like those of Bristol chassis, were restricted to state-owned companies. The first vehicle to be completed had a 70-seat rear-entrance body by Willowbrook of Loughborough and was delivered in the autumn of 1957 to Blue Bus of Willington, near Derby. This bus would enjoy a long operating life, finally being withdrawn in 1977 by Derby Borough Transport, which had taken over the Blue Bus business in 1973.

The first major order for the Loline came from loyal Dennis supporter Aldershot & District, which took 34 with 68-seat rear-entrance East Lancs bodies in 1958, making it briefly the biggest operator of low-height buses outside the BTC and Scottish groups. The company would later describe its original Lolines as 'most satisfactory and economical'. There were only five other Loline deliveries in 1958. A second Willowbrook-bodied bus joined the Blue Bus fleet, while Somerset independent Hutchings & Cornelius took an East Lancs-bodied bus, similar to the vehicles supplied to Aldershot & District; it operated on the company's service between South Petherton and Yeovil.

The three other 1958 deliveries broke new ground for Dennis, going to two small municipal fleets which had problems with low bridges. Leigh Corporation took two, with East Lancs bodies, while one with a Northern Counties body went to Middlesbrough Corporation. This was an exhibit at the 1958 Commercial Motor Show. Leigh placed a repeat order for a second pair, delivered in 1959. Britain's biggest independent, Lancashire United Transport, which in the late 1940s had bought 19 lowbridge Lances, took two Northern Counties-bodied Lolines in 1959 and four more in 1960. At this time most of LUT's double-deckers were Guy Arabs. Although non-standard in the LUT fleet the Lolines were operated for 13 years.

Production of the AEC/Park Royal Bridgemaster got underway in late 1958, and the first deliveries, in the winter of 1958/9, were 20 for Western Welsh. These were short 27ft 8in models and seated 68. They were accompanied by four 30ft 72-seaters for sister BET company South Wales Transport. SWT would add another five Bridgemasters later in 1959. Both operators were established AEC customers, operating Regents and Reliances. Also delivered at this time were six for Sheffield Transport with 76 seats – an unusually high capacity for a front-engined bus. One of the Sheffield buses was exhibited at the 1958 Commercial Motor Show. The following year one of the Western Welsh buses featured in an AEC advertisement which promoted the Bridgemaster as 'one vehicle for low bridge and normal routes,' hailing it as 'a triumph of advanced design – the first all-route double-decker in existence'.

A fourth Bridgemaster demonstrator, 116 TMD, was supplied in 1959 to Liverpool Corporation, entering service in January, initially on loan, before being purchased in October. It was trialled alongside a forward-entrance Regent V and an Atlantean. AEC had long been a supplier of buses to Liverpool, having delivered Regents regularly since the 1930s. However, the Bridgemaster was to be Liverpool's last AEC; when the city placed orders for new buses in the 1960s it chose Leylands.

BELOW: An artist's impression was used to add colour to an early Bridgemaster brochure, which included an image based on the original Crossley-designed prototypes.
Ian Allan Library

Three other municipal customers – Grimsby-Cleethorpes, Leicester and Southend – took two Bridgemasters each in 1959. Southend, like Loline buyers Leigh and Middlesbrough, had a low bridge to deal with, and had been buying lowbridge Leyland Titans. The Grimsby-Cleethorpes buses were short 68-seaters and followed a batch of Regent Vs delivered in 1957. At Leicester, as at Grimsby-Cleethorpes, there was no particular issue with bridge clearances, but the low floor of the Bridgemaster was seen as a way of reducing the time it took people to board and alight, because it eliminated the step into the lower saloon.

The first independent to buy a Bridgemaster was King Alfred of Winchester, which received a pair of 74-seaters in the autumn of 1959. They were the company's first new AECs and joined a predominantly Leyland fleet. At the end of 1959 AEC produced another Bridgemaster demonstrator, 80 WMH, its fifth. It would be sold to Osborne of Tollesbury in 1960.

Dennis was working on a revised Loline chassis, suitable for forward-entrance bodywork, and the

first example of what became the Loline II was delivered to Walsall Corporation in 1958, with a 70-seat Willowbrook body. It would be 1960 before any more Loline IIs were built.

At the close of the 1950s AEC and Dennis had between them built 95 of their low-height models – 50 Bridgemasters and 45 Lolines. The AEC total included five demonstrators, so in terms of new sales to actual customers the two manufacturers were equal. But to put these 95 buses in perspective, there were well over 1,000 examples of the original low-height bus, the Lodekka, in service by the end of the decade.

Leyland had for the time being abandoned low-height buses. It was selling Titans with lowbridge bodies in large numbers to the Scottish Bus Group and in smaller numbers elsewhere. And it was also selling lowbridge Atlanteans, which had conventional two-plus-two seating at the front of the upper deck but a side gangway at the rear. This odd arrangement was needed to provide headroom in the lower deck, where the gangway stepped up to clear the rear axle. Most lowbridge Atlanteans were bought by BET-group companies.

LEFT: The first five Bridgemasters had attractive Crossley-designed aluminium-framed bodywork, and this bus, vehicle number 002, carries a Crossley badge. It would be registered 9 JML and after a period as a demonstrator would be sold to Birmingham Corporation. It is seen outside the AEC factory in Windmill Lane, Southall. AEC

BELOW: The first Bridgemaster to enter service was vehicle 001, which joined the Walsall Corporation fleet at the end of 1956. It carried a Crossley badge, and its Crossley body seated 72. The sliding door for the driver's cab was relatively unusual at this time outside London but was a standard Bridgemaster feature. Geoffrey Morant

LEFT: Bridgemaster No 003 was registered 60 MMD and served as a demonstrator, as seen here in service in Sheffield in 1957. The first two Bridgemasters had flush-mounted glazing; this one uses standard Park Royal window pans. Daniel Hill collection

BELOW: In 1960 Bridgemaster 003 joined the South Wales Transport fleet, where it ran until 1969. This is a 1967 view, at Neath. Geoffrey Morant

RIGHT: The fourth Bridgemaster demonstrator entered service in 1957 and was subsequently purchased by Barton Transport. It is seen outside Barton's Chilwell offices in 1963. Geoff Mills

BELOW: Belfast Corporation's livery showed off to good effect the attractive lines of the Crossley body. This bus, Bridgemaster 005, entered service in 1958. It was supplied as a part-built structure which was finished by Belfast's local bodybuilder, Harkness, demonstrating an awareness by ACV of local sensitivities about preserving employment. It ran for Belfast until 1970. Geoffrey Morant

ABOVE: For a 1956 specification leaflet Dennis was clearly at a loss when it came to an illustration of the new Loline, coming up with this drawing of a quaint lowbridge bus with six-bay bodywork of a style which might just have passed for modern 20 years earlier. Ian Allan Library

BELOW: This drawing of a Loline chassis shows clearly the drop-centre rear axle with the differential located towards the offside. This is a Loline II, on which the chassis frame has been modified to accommodate forward-entrance bodywork. Ian Allan Library

ABOVE: By 1957 — and still before it had actually built any Lolines — Dennis used a photograph of a Lodekka to promote its new model which it was building under licence from Bristol. The image was re-touched to feature a Dennis grille. The advert claims: 'The Dennis Loline is an outstanding achievement of up-to-date design and engineering.' Stewart J. Brown collection

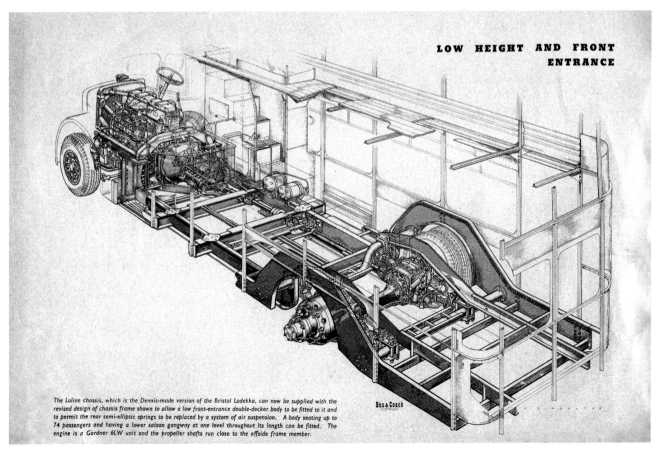

The Loline chassis, which is the Dennis-made version of the Bristol Lodekka, can now be supplied with the revised design of chassis frame shown to allow a low front-entrance double-decker body to be fitted to it and to permit the rear semi-elliptic springs to be replaced by a system of air suspension. A body seating up to 74 passengers and having a lower saloon gangway at one level throughout its length can be fitted. The engine is a Gardner 6LW unit and the propeller shafts run close to the offside frame member.

ABOVE: The first Dennis Loline to enter service did so with Blue Bus of Willington. The bus was completed in November 1957 and briefly acted as a Dennis demonstrator before entering service with Blue Bus in the early months of 1958. It had a 70-seat Willowbrook body and was followed by a second identical bus in 1958. Blue Bus needed lowbridge or low-height buses to clear a railway bridge in Willington. After the two Lolines its next new double-decker, in 1960, was a lowbridge Daimler CVG6. Roy Marshall

BELOW: The Blue Bus Lolines passed to Derby Corporation when the latter purchased the independent operator in 1973. Pictured in Derby in 1974 is the same vehicle illustrated above. It operated for Derby until 1977. Stewart J. Brown

RIGHT: Aldershot & District had bought 72 Dennis Lances with lowbridge bodies in the late 1940s and early 1950s and switched to the Loline in 1958. This was the first fleet order for the new Dennis model and comprised 34 buses with 68-seat bodies by East Lancs. Aldershot & District was easily the biggest user of the original Loline, taking all but 14 of the 48 produced. John May

BELOW: The Dennis Loline – like the Lodekka from which it was derived – had a rearward-facing seat against the front bulkhead. This is one of Aldershot & District's 1957 East Lancs-bodied buses. Ian Allan Library

RIGHT: An East Lancs-bodied Loline similar to those for Aldershot & District was purchased by Hutchings & Cornelius of South Petherton, Somerset, in 1958. It was operated until 1973, when it was replaced by a Bristol VRT. Roy Marshall

LEFT: The first Dennises for Leigh Corporation were four Lolines with 72-seat East Lancs bodies, delivered in pairs in 1958 and 1959. This was a 1959 bus, which, like all of the first series of Lolines, had a Gardner 6LW engine. Roy Marshall

LEFT: Middlesbrough Corporation's first Loline was a Commercial Motor Show exhibit in 1958, although the glitz of the show had long since faded by the time of this photograph. The bus was fitted with Cave-Browne-Cave heating, with twin radiators alongside the destination display. The well-proportioned 67-seat body was by Northern Counties, the Wigan builder's first on a low-height chassis. Nicholas Harris / Don Akrigg

RIGHT: Six Northern Counties-bodied Lolines were purchased by Lancashire United Transport in 1959/60. They were 69-seaters. The design of the low-height body precluded the use of LUT's standard three-section destination and route-number display; there would usually have been a third panel for the final destination below the two-piece display seen on this bus, inside the company's Atherton depot. These were the last of the original Loline model; in 1960 production switched to the Loline II. Geoffrey Morant

LEFT: Series production of Bridgemasters at Park Royal started towards the end of 1958, and among the first were 20 short models for Western Welsh, most of which entered service in the first few months of 1959. They were 68-seaters. The steel-framed Park Royal body lacked the elegance of the Crossley prototypes. This is Cardiff bus station. The adverts flanking the destination display promote Western Welsh coach hire. Geoffrey Morant

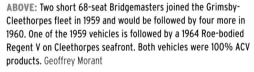

BELOW: A Bridgemaster demonstrator was operated by Liverpool Corporation from the start of 1959 and was purchased later in that year. It was numbered E3 in a series of experimental vehicles, the other two being a 30ft-long forward-entrance AEC Regent V and a Leyland Atlantean. Liverpool had a long history of buying AEC double-deckers, but this Bridgemaster would be its last. British Commercial Vehicle Museum

ABOVE: Two short 68-seat Bridgemasters joined the Grimsby-Cleethorpes fleet in 1959 and would be followed by four more in 1960. One of the 1959 vehicles is followed by a 1964 Roe-bodied Regent V on Cleethorpes seafront. Both vehicles were 100% ACV products. Geoffrey Morant

RIGHT: Leicester also purchased two Bridgemasters in 1959, but opted for the 30ft-long version with 72 seats. Another four followed in 1960. Here a 1959 bus receives a wash in the operator's garage; two of the identical 1960 buses can be seen in the background on the right, while on the left is a Regent III. The unusual numberplate location kept the plate out of harm's way in the event of a minor collision. AEC

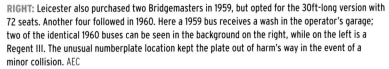

ABOVE: Southend operated six Bridgemasters – two delivered in 1959, and four in 1960. They were maximum-capacity 76-seaters, an impressive figure for a 30ft-long front-engined bus; vehicles of this size more commonly seated 70 or 72. Note the comprehensive destination display. Roy Marshall

BELOW: The first independent customer for the Bridgemaster was King Alfred Motor Services, of Winchester, which took delivery of a pair in 1959. They were the company's first new AECs and joined a double-deck fleet made up of 16 Leyland Titans, most with lowbridge bodies, and an ex-demonstration Regent V. Stewart J. Brown

ABOVE: Dennis was in the lead in developing a low-height chassis suitable for forward-entrance bodywork, which was becoming increasingly popular following the 1956 changes in the law which permitted 30ft-long double-deckers. It built this prototype Loline II for Walsall Corporation in 1958 and exhibited it at that year's Commercial Motor Show. Bristol's first forward-entrance Lodekka, the FLF, was launched in 1959, while AEC's forward-entrance Bridgemaster did not appear until 1960. It would be 1960 before Dennis switched to Loline II production.
Roy Marshall

RIGHT: This cut-away drawing was used by Leyland in its Atlantean advertising and shows how the rearmost four rows of seats on the top deck are located on a raised platform with access from a nearside gangway. It produced a bus with an overall height of 13ft 4in, according to the advert, and avoided the complexity and cost of a drop-centre rear axle.
The main user of lowbridge Atlanteans was the BET group.
Stewart J. Brown collection

Leyland 'ATLANTEAN'
73-seater *or* 78-seater
(*unladen height 13'4"*) (*unladen height 14'4"*)

LEYLAND MOTORS LTD. Home Sales Office: 3 LYGON PLACE, LONDON, S.W.1. Telephone: SLOane 6117
Export Division: HANOVER HOUSE, HANOVER SQUARE, LONDON, W.1. Telephone: MAYfair 8561

Chapter Two

THE MOVE TO FORWARD ENTRANCES

ABOVE: A production West Riding Wulfrunian shows the plain front panel, with slots to provide some airflow around the engine; those on the nearside are ornamental. There was no conventional radiator, as the buses were fitted with Cave-Browne-Cave heating, the grilles flanking the destination screen providing cool air for the system. This 1961 bus shows clearly the nearside staircase and the use of narrow leaves on the rear section of the door to minimise obstruction of the area at the foot of the stairs when the doors were open. Stewart J. Brown collection

ABOVE: The first Guy Wulfrunian was completed in 1959 and, like most of those that followed, had bodywork by Roe of Leeds, the preferred bodybuilder of West Riding, which operator was heavily involved in the model's development. It started life with this so-called butterfly-style grille; subsequent Wulfrunians had utilitarian horizontal slots in the front panel – a low-cost engineering solution which seemed strangely at odds with such a sophisticated piece of automotive design. The butterfly grille on this bus was later replaced by plain slotted panels. It is seen in Leeds in the red and cream livery used by West Riding for vehicles employed on former tram services. Robert F. Mack

The most dramatic approach to a low-height bus came from Guy – the Wulfrunian. This appeared in 1959 and copied the layout of the Atlantean in terms of its 30ft length and set-back front wheels. And there any resemblance to the Leyland model ended. The Wulfrunian had its engine at the front, a 10.45-litre Gardner 6LX, offset to the offside by around 16 inches to maximise platform space. There were other engine options – the smaller Gardner 6LW, Leyland's O.600 and O.680 and the AEC AV590. However, as it turned out, all Wulfrunians were Gardner-powered.

Most double-deck buses at this time still had manual gearboxes, and the Wulfrunian was offered with the choice of a ZF manual gearbox or a Guy-built semi-automatic. The use of Cave-Browne-Cave heating, with twin radiators at upper-deck floor level, eliminated the conventional radiator, further helping to save space at the front. The bus had a rearward-ascending staircase located over the front nearside wheel, along with advanced features such as air suspension, independent on the front wheels, and Girling air-hydraulic disc brakes. A prototype was bodied by Roe for West Riding in 1959, and in the spring of 1960 the company's chairman was able to report that it had been 'exceptionally well received by the travelling public'. It was followed in 1960 by two demonstrators for Guy and the first of a batch of 25 production vehicles for West Riding. The first 12 were delivered

between November 1960 and January 1961, the balance following in the spring of 1961. By the end of 1961 West Riding would have received another 25, taking its fleet to 51. When new the prototype had a butterfly-style grille, but this was later replaced by a plain and rather unattractive panel with horizontal cooling slats cut into it, as fitted to most Wulfrunians.

Lancashire United and Bury Corporation each took one Wulfrunian in 1960, and both operators' buses were exhibits at the 1960 Commercial Motor Show. The LUT vehicle was the only Wulfrunian to be bodied by Northern Counties, and in 1962 it was sold to West Riding. LUT had in fact ordered three but cancelled the other two. The Bury bus lasted marginally longer with its original owner but was sold in 1963. The only other 1960 deliveries were a pair for County Motors of Lepton, a company in which West Riding had an interest. The County buses were transferred to the West Riding fleet in 1963, being replaced by two Leyland Titan PD3As.

The two Wulfrunian demonstrators, 7800 DA and 8072 DA, in a distinctive yellow livery, travelled far and wide to such diverse fleets as Western SMT, Belfast Corporation, Glasgow Corporation and Southdown. Belfast actually ordered one Wulfrunian but soon had a change of heart and cancelled it. The first of the demonstrators was road-tested by *Commercial Motor* magazine in August 1960, when just a few weeks old. The tester, John F. Moon, noted that 'many potential operators may doubt whether the apparent complication of the chassis would be justified in service', before continuing: 'After an exclusive road test of this outstanding, but not expensive, vehicle, I can set their minds at rest.' Hindsight would show that Mr Moon was a bit hasty in his reassurance.

The test vehicle weighed just over 8½ tons unladen. When carrying test weights to represent a full load of passengers it returned fuel consumption figures of 5.9mpg when making six stops a mile to simulate urban operation and 12.4mpg on non-stop running.

Both Wulfrunian demonstrators were later sold to West Riding, where they were used as a source of spare parts.

The 1960s started well for Dennis, and its forward-entrance Loline II secured an impressive 47 sales, most of which were delivered in 1960. Walsall, which had taken the prototype Loline II in 1958, added another 16, all bodied by Willowbrook. Middlesbrough, which had bought a solitary Loline in 1958, took eight Loline IIs which had unusual full-fronted Northern Counties bodies. And yet another municipal with a lowbridge requirement, Luton Corporation, turned to Dennis, for a pair of East Lancs-bodied Loline IIs. These had a short wheelbase (16ft 8½in rather than 19ft) and were 63-seaters, at a time when a standard 30ft-long Loline II seated between 70 and 74. They had Leyland O.600 engines, providing a measure of commonality with the Leyland Titans in the Luton fleet, and cost £3,310 each.

Two more BET companies decided to try Lolines, following Aldershot & District's lead. North Western took 15, with East Lancs bodies and a mixture of Leyland O.600 and Gardner 6LX engines. But more interesting was City of Oxford Motor Services, with five. COMS was a staunch AEC customer. In 1960 all of its double-deckers were AEC Regents, so the order represented quite a coup for Dennis, which was no doubt happy to fit AEC engines – the only Lolines to be so equipped. And it must have been an irritation for ACV, which might reasonably have anticipated supplying Oxford with five complete buses, not just five engines. It was to be a brief success for Dennis; from 1961 City of Oxford reverted to AEC, starting with 10 Bridgemasters.

Oxford's Lolines, like those for Luton, were short models and had similar 63-seat East Lancs bodies.

One final Loline II was built in 1960 and exhibited at that year's Commercial Motor Show. It was for Barton Transport and had a stylish 68-seat full-front lowbridge Northern Counties body with curved windscreens. Its overall height was just 12ft 6in making it Britain's lowest-ever double-decker. It entered service in 1961. Total Loline II production was 48, including the one pre-production bus supplied to Walsall in 1958.

Dennis advertising of this time in *Bus & Coach* magazine provides a commentary on engine

TOP AND BOTTOM: Two demonstration Wulfrunians were built in 1960. One is seen in service with Western SMT in Kilmarnock, where it must have made some impression with its forward-entrance layout – novel on a double-decker at that time – and bright-yellow livery; the destination display promotes the use of air suspension. The other is in the demonstration park at the 1960 Commercial Motor Show at Earl's Court and shows clearly the nearside staircase. The fitting of twin headlights was unusual on a double-deck bus. Gavin Booth collection, Geoffrey Morant

ABOVE: The Wulfrunian was an odd choice for Bury Corporation. It joined a fleet made up overwhelmingly of Leyland Titans, and where the only Guys ever operated had been two light Wolf models in the early 1950s. The Roe body had extra style, with attractive trim to conceal the Cave-Browne-Cave air intakes. The bus was exhibited at the 1960 Commercial Motor Show before being delivered to Bury. It was short-lived, being sold in 1963. Peter Roberts

availability. In 1959 the company was still promoting its own engine alongside the Gardner 6LW. In 1960 the Dennis engine was no longer mentioned, and the advertised options were Gardner 5LW, 6LW and 6LX, Leyland O.600 and O.680 and AEC AV470 and AV590 – a total of seven different engines ranging in size from the 5LW's 7 litres to the 11.1 litres of the O.680. But in the following year just two engines were listed – the 6LW and the 6LX.

The Loline III was a development of the Loline II and was easily identifiable by a new and perhaps less harmonious grille. It was offered with a semi-automatic transmission, an option not previously available. A chassis was exhibited at the 1960 Commercial Motor Show, and the first Loline IIIs entered service in 1961. They included a follow-on order from North Western, for 15 with Alexander bodies. There were also two for Leigh, its last. These were unusual in having rear-entrance bodywork, the only bodies of this layout on the Loline III.

Other early Loline III business included one bus for Belfast Corporation and the first Loline export order, for China Motor Bus in Hong Kong. Both of these buses had Northern Counties bodies, and

that for Belfast was the first Loline to be fitted with a semi-automatic gearbox. It was in the demonstration park at the 1960 Commercial Motor Show. It was part of the Corporation's programme of evaluating potential buses for the future and joined a 1958 Bridgemaster and a 1960 Atlantean. It was to be the only forward-entrance half-cab double-decker in the fleet. When Belfast placed a bulk order for new buses in 1962 these came not from AEC, Leyland or Dennis but from Daimler.

AEC, like Dennis, recognised the need for a forward-entrance version of its low-height bus and developed a revised Bridgemaster, the 2B3RA, the first of which were five delivered to South Wales Transport in the spring of 1960. A 2B3RA was built for AEC's demonstration fleet at the same time – the sixth and final Bridgemaster demonstrator, 2211 MK. It spent the best part of a year, from mid-1960 to mid-1961, running for Birmingham City Transport and then joined one of its rear-entrance predecessors in the Osborne fleet in Essex.

To create a forward-entrance version of the Bridgemaster was a major engineering exercise. The driveline was revised and once again featured a transfer box at the rear of the gearbox and changes to the nearside of the front subframe. A step-free entrance was no longer possible, and forward-entrance Bridgemasters had a shallow (5$\frac{1}{2}$in) internal step. On the original, rear-entrance Bridgemaster a rearward-facing seat for five passengers was located behind the front bulkhead, covering the gearbox. This was clearly not possible on the revised model, on which the gearbox intruded into the saloon, and in consequence the doorway was located about 18 inches behind the bulkhead. This odd layout did at least create a space for the conductor to stand, between the bulkhead and the foot of the forward-ascending staircase.

AEC's 1960 brochure for the new model noted: 'The Bridgemaster dispenses with the need for both normal and low-height vehicles in one fleet, with obvious advantages in vehicle availability, and indeed its many advantages and modern suspension will appeal to operators to whom low height is not essential. Only minor changes to the mechanical units by the introduction of a transfer box at the rear of the gearbox have been necessary for the front-entrance model.'

All of the other 1960 Bridgemasters were rear-entrance models. There were repeat orders from Southend and Grimsby-Cleethorpes, with four buses each, while Cardiff Corporation had six. Both Cardiff and Grimsby-Cleethorpes specified short versions. BET subsidiary East Yorkshire, which company's last new double deckers had been Regent Vs in 1957, also took four Bridgemasters in 1960, having previously evaluated one of the demonstrators.

In 1961 the forward-entrance Bridgemaster gained ground, 27 being delivered to six operators. There was a repeat order from South Wales, for eight, while City of Oxford took ten, its first, after the batch of Lolines earlier in the year. Sheffield, which had taken six rear-entrance Bridgemasters in 1959, added a solitary forward-entrance bus to its fleet. Nearby Rotherham took five, to replace single-deck trolleybuses on a route operated jointly with the Mexborough & Swinton Traction Co; Mexborough & Swinton, a BET subsidiary, used lowbridge Atlanteans for its share of the service. And three were delivered to two Scottish independents which normally bought lowbridge

BELOW: The only Wulfrunian to be bodied by Northern Counties was that for Lancashire United Transport. It entered service at the end of 1960 but after little more than 12 months was sold to West Riding. The 1930s Quarry Hill flats provide the backdrop to this view in Leeds.
Geoffrey Morant

Leyland Titans, two going to Smith of Barrhead and one to Baxter's of Airdrie.

There were rear-entrance Bridgemaster deliveries too, three fleets between them taking 23 in 1961. The biggest buyer was East Yorkshire, with a repeat order for 16; these and subsequent Bridgemasters for the company differed from the four delivered in 1960 in that the upper-deck pillars were canted inward to allow the buses to pass through the arch of the North Bar in Beverley. There was also repeat business from Leicester (five buses) and King Alfred (two).

At the start of the 1960s Guy was struggling to find new customers for the Wulfrunian. Wolverhampton Corporation supported its local bus manufacturer with an order for one East Lancs-bodied vehicle which was delivered in 1961, alongside 30 Arab IVs. Accrington Corporation, which, like Wolverhampton, ran Guy Arabs, took two Wulfrunians. These too were bodied by East Lancs, and were the only Wulfrunians to have rear entrances. These were based on the optional shorter chassis, which had a 16ft 4in wheelbase for bodywork of around 28ft in length. They also had 6LW engines rather than the bigger 6LX, which was fitted to all other Wulfrunians, and the engines were fitted in the centre line of the chassis rather than being offset to the offside – a design feature unnecessary when there was no need to provide space for an entrance. They were both withdrawn in 1968 when their initial Certificates of Fitness expired and briefly saw service with other operators before being scrapped in 1971. The seven-year lives of the Wulfrunians in Accrington's fleet contrasted with 15 years for the operator's Arabs.

Independent West Wales of Tycroes had one Wulfrunian, also bodied by East Lancs, being sufficiently proud of it to enter it in the 1961 Brighton Coach Rally. But such pride was short-lived, as was the bus. It was sold in 1962 to West Riding, where it was operated until 1969. It was the only new Wulfrunian for a Welsh operator.

AEC and Dennis had pursued a conventional approach to low-height buses, retaining a front engine. Guy had retained a front engine but designed an entirely new bus around it. Leyland had temporarily given up on the concept, relying on lowbridge bodies on its Atlantean. Which left Daimler. And Daimler's solution was the only truly successful one – the Fleetline, with a rear engine and a drop-centre rear axle. It was launched in 1960. And its success means it doesn't fit alongside the low-volume models featured here.

At the end of 1961 Leyland, under pressure from the Scottish Bus Group, which wanted to stop buying Titan PD3s with lowbridge bodies, reluctantly adopted a new approach to the challenge of low-height buses. The new model, the Albion Lowlander, was launched at the 1961 Scottish Motor Show in the shape of an Alexander-bodied bus for Western SMT.

The low-frame chassis was new, as was the drop-centre rear axle, which was later used in the low-height PDR1/2 Atlantean. There was a choice of Leyland's semi-automatic Pneumocyclic gearbox in the LR1 or the four-speed Leyland synchromesh in the LR3. The gearbox was mounted remotely, on the nearside of the chassis. Had it been bolted directly onto the back of the engine it would have intruded into the platform area, creating the same compromised entrance layout as AEC had with its forward-entrance Bridgemaster. Rear air suspension was soon offered as an option with the LR5 (Pneumocyclic) and LR7 (synchromesh). No LR5s were built.

To minimise development costs Leyland retained the front-end layout of the Titan, which meant a comparatively high-set driver's cab. The cab floor was 37 inches above the ground, compared with 33 inches for the floor in the Lodekka cab. Four inches might not sound much, but it forced compromises on the Alexander body, the four front seats on the upper deck being mounted higher than the rest. With Alexander's standard front dome there was room for only a single-line destination and route-number display on the first two completed vehicles – the bus for Western and a demonstrator in Glasgow Corporation livery.

SBG placed orders for 106 Lowlanders for delivery in 1962, although only 18 of these – ten for Central SMT and eight for Western – actually entered service that year. The rest followed in 1963 and included examples for the three Alexander companies – Fife, Midland and Northern. By this time a repeat order for 75 had been placed, for Central, Midland and Western. Some of the Lowlanders for Central and Western were bodied by Northern Counties, which dealt much more satisfactorily with the model's high driving position.

The Lowlander demonstrator, 747 EUS, operated on loan to Glasgow Corporation for 12 months from February 1962 – a strange decision by Leyland, for Glasgow had by then committed itself to the Atlantean, having placed an initial order for 150 in 1961. The bus was then repainted in Edinburgh Corporation colours and operated in that city in 1963, after which it was sold to Bamber Bridge Motor Services, of Preston. Edinburgh did in fact buy one Lowlander chassis. It was built in 1962 but was never used and was sold in 1965 to Western SMT, which had it bodied by Northern Counties.

In England the Lowlander was badged as a Leyland – a rare instance in the bus business of what was known as badge engineering, whereby a manufacturer sold what was effectively the same vehicle under two or more different brand names. The Albion name carried little weight as a double-deck bus outside Scotland (and, truth be told, not that much weight in Scotland either). Leyland produced two brochures which were nearly identical apart from the Albion or Leyland names. But, curiously, they showed different overall heights on a drawing on the front cover – 13ft 6in on the Leyland brochure but 13ft 4³/₈in on the Albion version. The first English order came from BET subsidiary East Midland, for 14 LR7s to be bodied by Alexander. The first of the East Midland Lowlanders was at the 1962 Commercial Motor Show, as was the first Northern Counties-bodied bus for Central SMT.

Two municipal fleets took Lowlanders in 1963. Sixteen went to Luton and had 65-seat East Lancs bodies. They followed two Leyland-engined Lolines delivered in 1960. For its next double-deckers, in 1965, Luton returned to Dennis. The other buyer was Southend Corporation, which specified Alexander bodywork on ten Lowlanders. They followed six Bridgemasters delivered in 1959/60. After the Lowlanders Southend reverted to Leyland PD3s. A third municipal, Walsall, had ordered 14 Lowlanders with MCW bodies in 1962 but later cancelled the order.

Only one independent bought new Lowlanders. South Notts of Gotham, which had been a Titan customer, took one Northern Counties-bodied bus each year for five years from 1963. Its last, in 1967, was the last Lowlander built.

At the end of 1962 West Riding received another batch of 20 Wulfrunians, but by this time it was clear that few other operators were interested in Guy's innovative but troublesome model. The only other 1962 delivery was a one-off for Wolverhampton Corporation with a shortened

ABOVE: Following the 1958 prototype forward-entrance Loline II Walsall Corporation took a batch of 16 production chassis in 1960, with 74-seat Willowbrook bodies. This one is seen in Dudley in the ownership of West Midlands PTE, which had taken over the Walsall operation in 1969. An Austin A40 follows. Geoffrey Morant

front overhang and the entrance behind the front axle. This layout matched the fleet's forward-entrance Arabs. It was the fifth (and last) Wulfrunian to be bodied by East Lancs and was a 1962 Commercial Motor Show exhibit. It took to just seven the number of Wulfrunians bought by operators other than West Riding or the associated County Motors business.

The Dennis Loline was doing well in 1962, with deliveries peaking at 76. This was due largely to two BET-group operators, Aldershot & District taking 48, and North Western 20. The Aldershot & District buses were part of two different orders. First came 20 Alexander-bodied buses, delivered in the winter of 1961/2 and at that time an unusually big order for the Scottish bodybuilder for double-deckers from an English operator. These were followed at the end of 1962 by 37 similar vehicles, delivery continuing into 1963.

Commercial Motor magazine carried out a road test of one of Aldershot & District's Alexander-bodied Loline IIIs with a Gardner 6LW engine and Dennis five-speed constant-mesh gearbox. The vehicle was fully laden, using test weights, and on a run with six stops per mile returned an impressive 9.25mpg. When cruising on the open road this rose to an incredible 15.7mpg.

There was some uncertainty surrounding Dennis's place in the bus business at this time. At the end of 1961 it had indicated that it was going to cease building bus chassis. Outstanding orders for Lolines were cancelled by three municipal fleets, Luton, Middlesbrough and Walsall – which helps explain Luton's Lowlander order. However Dennis still delivered just over 100 Lolines in 1961/2, and this may have prompted a rethink, because at the end of 1962 it announced a change of heart. But the uncertainty had created a hiatus which saw no Lolines entering service in 1963, and just four customers for the model after that – Reading, Aldershot & District, Luton and Halifax.

There was also a demonstrator, a chassis which had been bodied by Northern Counties in 1962, with the intention of exporting it to Hong Kong. It was not registered by Dennis until 1964, being exhibited in the demonstration park at that year's Commercial Motor Show. It was later purchased by Warner's of Tewkesbury.

BELOW: Middlesbrough Corporation had purchased one Loline in 1958 and followed it up with eight Loline IIs in 1960. These had full-front bodies by Northern Counties, with the short centre bay that was a feature of most of that builder's forward-entrance 30-footers. Note the municipal crest on both decks; also the use of a route letter rather than a number. This bus has Cave-Browne-Cave heating and a plain grille – there was no conventional radiator to cool.
Geoffrey Morant

LEFT: North Western, which in the 1950s had been buying lowbridge Leyland Titans, took 15 Loline IIs in 1960. These had 71-seat East Lancs bodies and were the operator's first forward-entrance double-deckers. Twelve had Leyland O.600 engines; the other three had Gardner 6LXs. The illuminated advertising display on the upper-deck side panels was briefly popular in the early 1960s and on this bus was promoting the company's Manchester–London service, on which the full journey took 5½ hours in each direction and cost 44s (£2.20) return. A 1961 Loline III stands alongside at North Western's Wilmslow depot. Arnold Richardson / Photobus

ABOVE: All of the double-deckers in the fleet of City of Oxford Motor Services were AEC Regents until five Dennis Loline IIs were delivered in 1961. These were at least fitted with an AEC engine, the 7.7-litre AV470, and were the only AEC-engined Lolines. East Lancs built the 63-seat bodies. The Oxford Mail is still published today. Geoffrey Morant

ABOVE: The centre of attraction on the Northern Counties stand at the 1960 Commercial Motor Show was the unique lowbridge Loline II for Barton Transport. Apart from the novelty of its record low overall height of 12ft 6in the curved glass windscreens made this bus stand out from other double-deckers at the show, most of which were either conventional half-cabs or box-like Atlanteans. Stewart J. Brown collection

ABOVE: The unusual lowbridge Loline II in service with Barton Transport, by which time a conventional radiator had replaced the original Cave-Browne-Cave installation. Roy Marshall

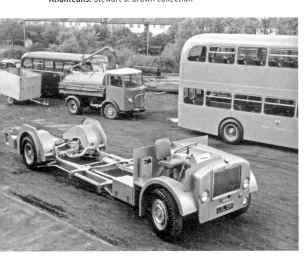

ABOVE: A Loline III chassis prepared for exhibition at the 1960 Commercial Motor Show. The bus partly visible on the right was another show exhibit, a Willowbrook-bodied Loline II for Walsall Corporation. Dennis

ABOVE: The first big orders for the Loline III came from the BET group. North Western took 15 in 1961 and for these specified 71-seat Alexander bodies. All had Gardner 6LX engines. A further 20 similar buses were delivered in 1962. A new, rectangular grille was used on the Loline III. Arnold Richardson / Photobus

LEFT: The biggest buyer of Alexander-bodied Lolines was Aldershot & District. One of the company's buses is seen under construction on the production lines of Alexander's factory in Falkirk. These were the first lowheight buses to be built by Alexander. A modified version of this body would be fitted to the Albion Lowlander chassis. R. H. G. Simpson

RIGHT: The only rear-entrance Loline IIIs were two delivered to Leigh Corporation in 1961. They had 72-seat bodywork by East Lancs. A. E. Jones

LEFT: Having bought one AEC Bridgemaster in 1958 and one Leyland Atlantean in 1960, Belfast Corporation bought one Dennis Loline III in 1961. It had a 76-seat Northern Counties body. Michael Dryhurst

RIGHT: A forward-entrance Bridgemaster demonstrator was built in 1960 and was operated by Birmingham City Transport for the best part of a year. It was then purchased by Osborne of Tollesbury, as seen here in Colchester bus station in June 1961, still in full Birmingham livery. Geoff Mills

ABOVE: Cardiff Corporation took six AEC Bridgemasters in 1960. They were short 68-seaters. Five were sold in 1972 to Newton of Dingwall, where they formed Scotland's biggest Bridgemaster fleet. Geoffrey Morant

LEFT: Another Welsh Bridgemaster customer in 1960 was South Wales Transport, which took five forward-entrance models. They followed nine rear-entrance buses delivered in 1959. This one is seen in Swansea in 1965. Geoff Mills

ABOVE: Following its Dennis Lolines City of Oxford reverted to its traditional chassis supplier, AEC, taking delivery of ten 72-seat forward-entrance Bridgemasters later in 1961. Note that the driver has only one step to gain access to the cab. You had to be agile to drive a Bridgemaster. John May

BELOW: To replace single-deck trolleybuses on a route with a low bridge Rotherham Corporation purchased five Bridgemasters in two batches in 1961. All were forward-entrance 70-seaters. Roy Marshall

THIS PAGE: Sheffield's solitary forward-entrance Bridgemaster, delivered in 1961, shows how the entrance was set back some 18 inches from the front bulkhead because the gearbox intruded into the platform area. On the original print of the pre-delivery photograph by Park Royal (left) the unladen weight of 8 tons 18cwt can be clearly read on the side of the vehicle. This was heavy by the standards of the time, being fully half a ton more than an equivalent FLF-type Bristol Lodekka. The bus was Sheffield's first forward-entrance double-decker and would be followed by 30ft-long Regent Vs to the same layout. Pictured subsequently in service in Sheffield (below), in 1969, it would be withdrawn in 1973.
Park Royal, Roy Marshall

ABOVE: The only short forward-entrance Bridgemasters were 13 for City of Oxford Motor Services. They entered service in the winter of 1962/3 and were easily identifiable by the unusually short foremost side window on the upper deck. This is a 1972 view of one of the buses near the end of its life in Oxford. Most of the batch – nine – were sold to Premiere Travel of Cambridge. Geoff Mills

BELOW: At the end of 1961 two Bridgemasters were delivered to Smith of Barrhead. Smith was owned by the Scottish Co-operative Wholesale Society and operated AEC Reliance coaches, but had hitherto been buying lowbridge Leyland Titans for its double-deck fleet. The Smith business was acquired by Western SMT in 1968. Iain MacGregor

ABOVE: Baxter's of Airdrie was running a smart fleet consisting mainly of AEC Reliances and lowbridge Leyland Titans when it took a Bridgemaster in 1961. The bus is seen in November of that year in the street which served as a demonstration park for the Scottish Motor Show in Glasgow's Kelvin Hall. It wore Baxter's smart colours for only a short time; in 1962 the company was taken over by Scottish Omnibuses. Iain MacGregor

BELOW: The last big order for rear-entrance Bridgemasters came from East Yorkshire, which took 16 in 1961. They were 73-seaters, and the bodywork was modified with the side pillars canted inwards above the upper-deck waist so that the buses could pass through the North Bar in Beverley; a feature of most East Yorkshire double-deck buses, this was commonly known as the 'Beverley Bar' roof. The buses had four-leaf platform doors and a destination display above the entrance. Roy Marshall

ABOVE: Alongside a batch of 30 ever-so-reliable Guy Arabs being delivered in 1961 Wolverhampton placed in service this Wulfrunian. It had a 72-seat East Lancs body. This picture gives some idea of the limited space for the driver; note the proximity of the steering wheel to the side of the body. Geoffrey Morant

LEFT: Among the most unusual Wulfrunians were two rear-entrance buses delivered to Accrington Corporation in 1961. These had a reduced front overhang and a Gardner 6LW engine located in the centre-line of the chassis. East Lancs built the 66-seat body and incorporated a Guy grille. These were the only Wulfrunians of this layout. Peter Roberts

72/74 seat double-deck bus chassis

Albion Lowlander

5'8½" headroom

13' 4½" overall height unladen

5' 10½" headroom

15½" to step

forward or rear entrance—single-level gangways lower & upper saloons

72/74 seat double-deck bus chassis

Leyland Lowlander

5'8½" headroom

13' 6" overall height unladen

5' 10½" headroom

15½" to step

forward or rear entrance—single-level gangways lower & upper saloons

ABOVE LEFT AND RIGHT: Leyland produced two brochures for the Lowlander — an Albion version for Scottish customers (just how many Scottish bus operators did Leyland think would be interested?) and a Leyland version for the rest of the UK. The illustration was not of a complete bus but an Alexander mock-up of the front end. The Lowlander lettering on the grille did not appear on production buses. Stewart J. Brown collection

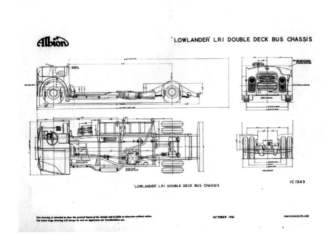

ABOVE: Albion produced detailed drawings to provide guidance for coachbuilders. This is an LR1 chassis drawing, dated October 1961. Stewart J. Brown

RIGHT: A Lowlander LR1 chassis, showing how the gearbox was located on the nearside, ahead of the rear axle. Stewart J. Brown collection

LEFT: The Lowlander was unveiled at the 1961 Scottish Motor Show, this bus in Western SMT livery being photographed outside the offices of bodybuilder Alexander before heading for Glasgow's Kelvin Hall exhibition centre. The raised front seats on the upper deck are clearly visible. There is an Albion badge on the flap giving access to the radiator filler, and a small Lowlander badge just above the numberplate. Albion

ABOVE: Leyland painted a Lowlander demonstrator in Glasgow Corporation livery, and it spent a year operating in the city. Glasgow was running a large fleet of forward-entrance Titan PD3s and had placed an order for 150 Atlanteans, so the Lowlander was something of an irrelevance. Iain MacGregor

ABOVE: After running in Glasgow for a year Leyland's Lowlander demonstrator was painted in an approximation of Edinburgh Corporation livery and spent some time in the Scottish capital. Iain MacGregor

BELOW: At the end of its demonstration period the Lowlander was sold to one of Leyland's local independents, Bamber Bridge Motor Services of Preston. Iain MacGregor

LEFT: In 1967 Bamber Bridge was taken over by Ribble, in which fleet the former demonstrator joined 16 other Lowlanders, although it remained immediately identifiable by virtue of its half-cab layout. Ribble did, however, fit the later style of Alexander front dome to make room for its standard destination display, as seen here in Wigan in 1974. Stewart J. Brown

RIGHT: Northern Counties did not have as much trouble as Alexander in developing a body for the Lowlander, as this Central SMT bus, which had been an exhibit at the 1962 Commercial Motor Show, illustrates. Central had 20 Lowlanders with Northern Counties bodies. Harry Hay

LEFT: Production Alexander bodies for the Lowlander had a revised front dome with the windows raised to accommodate the Scottish Bus Group's standard destination display, as seen on this Western SMT bus in Irvine. This modification also improved forward vision for front-seat passengers. On this bus only the offside front seat is raised, which it had to be to clear the driver's cab; the nearside seat is at the same level as the rest of those on the upper deck. Stewart J. Brown

RIGHT: Alexander (Midland) had 44 Lowlanders, all bodied by Alexander and delivered in 1963/4. The company was at the same time buying FLF Lodekkas, but in 1967 it would switch to rear-engined Daimler Fleetlines. Stewart J. Brown

LEFT: The first English Lowlanders were 14 Alexander-bodied buses for East Midland Motor Services, and these entered service in the early months of 1963. They carried Leyland names on the grille but retained the Albion badge on the radiator filler flap. The low entrance is clearly visible in this view in Nottingham in 1970. Roy Marshall

ABOVE: The only Lowlanders to be bodied by East Lancs were 16 delivered to Luton Corporation in the summer of 1963. They were 65-seaters and were built on standard-wheelbase chassis but with a shortened rear overhang. Geoffrey Morant

ABOVE: Southend Corporation was the only other municipal Lowlander buyer, taking ten Alexander-bodied buses in 1963. The revised front dome left just enough room for the operator's comprehensive destination display, although prospective passengers would need good eyesight to be able to read the names of the six intermediate points listed. Geoffrey Morant

RIGHT: Just one independent bought new Lowlanders. This was South Notts of Gotham, which took five, one being purchased each year from 1963 to 1967. They were LR3s with manual gearboxes and conventional springs on the rear axle, a relatively uncommon specification. They had Northern Counties bodies which were similar to those supplied to the Scottish Bus Group, the only other buyer of Northern Counties-bodied Lowlanders, but with a sliding door rather than the double-jacknife design favoured by SBG. Roy Marshall

LEFT: A second Wulfrunian joined the Wolverhampton fleet at the end of 1962, having been exhibited at that year's Commercial Motor Show. Like Accrington's two buses it had a shortened front overhang and an East Lancs body, but with the entrance located behind the front wheel. In this view it is seen near the end of its life, running for West Midlands PTE, which had taken over the Wolverhampton operation in 1969. The headache advertisement seems apt for a Wulfrunian. Geoffrey Morant

ABOVE: East Yorkshire switched from rear to forward entrances for its 1962 and 1963 Bridgemasters but retained the modified upper-deck profile needed for them to operate through the North Bar at Beverley. The last Bridgemasters of all would be 15 delivered to East Yorkshire in the spring of 1963. Roy Marshall

ABOVE: This Loline had been built in 1962 for Hong Kong but never made the trip. Fitted with a Northern Counties body, it appeared in the demonstration park at the 1964 Commercial Motor Show and was subsequently registered by Dennis. It was later sold to Warner's of Tewkesbury. Harry Hay

ABOVE: In its 1964 advertising to coincide with the Commercial Motor Show Dennis claimed that the Loline was so economical that it was the equivalent of getting a free bus in every batch ordered. Were 1960s bus buyers naïve enough to believe such a vague and unsubstantiated claim? Probably not. There would be only one new Loline customer after this advert appeared — Halifax, in 1967. Stewart J. Brown collection

Chapter Three
THE END OF THE COMPETITORS

ABOVE: One rear-entrance Bridgemaster was purchased by Red Rover of Aylesbury. A 76-seater, it was delivered in 1962 and operated until 1977. This photograph was taken when the bus was new, with an earlier and more elegant generation of AEC double-decker in the background, in the shape of an ex-London Transport RT-class Regent III. Geoff Mills

ABOVE: Red Rover later received a forward-entrance Bridgemaster, which was one of a pair that had been ordered by Baxter's of Airdrie. It was delivered in 1963.
Geoff Mills

Rear-entrance buses were falling from favour in the early 1960s, and the last rear-entrance Bridgemasters were built in 1962. There were eight in all – a further three for Leicester (taking its fleet to ten), four for Lincoln and one for Red Rover of Aylesbury. Forward-entrance models were delivered to three BET companies. East Yorkshire received 15, while East Kent (which had settled on the Regent V as its preferred double-decker) took three for a town service in Dover. An order for 13 for City of Oxford, its second and last batch of Bridgemasters, was delivered at the end of 1962, entering service in December and in January 1963. These were 28ft 6in-long 65-seaters and were the only short forward-entrance Bridgemasters built.

Baxter's of Airdrie had ordered another two Bridgemasters, shortly before the business was purchased by Scottish Omnibuses at the end of 1962. One was taken into the Scottish Omnibuses fleet; the second was sold to Red Rover of Aylesbury. Both entered service in 1963. The final Bridgemasters were 15 for East Yorkshire, delivered in the spring of 1963 and giving the company the biggest fleet of the model, with 50. They brought total production to 180 – 99 rear-entrance and 81 forward-entrance. Most went to English operators; there were 48 new Bridgemasters in Wales, and

just four in Scotland. The BET group was the biggest customer, with 118, or 65% of production, these being shared between five operators – City of Oxford, East Kent, East Yorkshire, South Wales and Western Welsh.

The Bridgemaster's replacement was the Renown, reviving a name last used by AEC in the 1930s for a three-axle double-decker. This featured a separate chassis, giving buyers the freedom to choose their own bodybuilder. As *Bus & Coach* magazine noted, 'Consequently it is likely to meet with the approval of a wider circle of bus undertakings.' It was designed to the newly authorised maximum width of 8ft 2½in and had the same engine as the Bridgemaster, the 9.6-litre AV590, but unlike the Bridgemaster had a beam front axle. One plus-point of the Renown was the availability of AEC's Monocontrol semi-automatic gearbox as an alternative to the synchromesh unit which had been standard on the Bridgemaster. The synchromesh gearbox was conventionally located directly behind the engine on the 3B3RA model, but the semi-automatic 3B2RA had its gearbox located slightly further back in the chassis, dictating a different staircase layout depending upon the type of gearbox specified.

Two pre-production demonstrators – bodied by Park Royal, ACV's in-house bodybuilder – were built in 1962. One, 8071 ML, painted in the dark green of London Transport's Country Area, was in the demonstration park at the 1962 Commercial Motor Show. Built with 75 seats, it was downseated to 69 and spent a few months running for London Transport at Northfleet, in Kent, in 1963. It was then returned to AEC and was sold to Osborne of Tollesbury at the end of that year. The other demonstrator, 7552 MX, was tried by operators around Britain before being sold in 1965 to Burwell & District, which operated it until 1977. Among the operators to evaluate it was Halifax, where it returned a fuel-consumption figure of 9.15mpg. It was also the subject of a road test in *Passenger Transport* magazine, wherein it was described by tester Alan Townsin as 'a generally rather unsophisticated but robust machine'. Fully laden and with four stops per mile it returned fuel economy of 8.4mpg, this rising to 13.4mpg in non-stop running on the open road.

The first production Renowns to enter service were 14 with Park Royal bodies for South Wales Transport, delivered in the spring of 1963 at the same time as the last Bridgemasters were joining the East Yorkshire fleet. An SWT Renown featured in AEC's advertising, which quaintly asserted that it was 'offering probably the highest degree ever achieved in passenger comfort with orthodox seating' – implying that there was perhaps somewhere a more comfortable bus with unorthodox seating. Later in the year SWT received another five Renowns, but bodied by Willowbrook. Only six Renowns would have Willowbrook bodies – the five SWT buses plus one for West Wales.

There were other significant Renown deliveries to BET companies in 1963, North Western taking 18, as it switched its business from Dennis to AEC, and ten going to City of Oxford, where the Renown was the natural successor to the company's two batches of Bridgemasters. Both North Western and City of Oxford specified Park Royal bodies. The Oxford buses were short 65-seaters.

Leigh Corporation, which was running six Dennis Lolines, switched back to the Leyland Titan with lowbridge bodywork for the two vehicles it bought in 1962, then moved on to the Renown in 1963, taking four with rear-entrance East Lancs bodies. It then standardised on the Renown, taking another 14 East Lancs-bodied buses, but with forward entrances, in the period 1964-7. These were the undertaking's last double-deckers. Among the buses they replaced were lowbridge AEC Regent IIIs from the late 1940s.

While Dennis lost out at Leigh it did win at Reading. Most of Reading's motor buses were AECs when it took eight Loline IIIs with handsome East

Lancs bodies in 1962. More would follow, and by the time the last entered service in 1966 there were 26 in the fleet.

Aldershot & District received 50 Lolines in 1964/5, and these had Weymann rather than Alexander bodies. The chassis cost £168,000, according to contemporary press reports – equal to £3,360 each. One completed bus was exhibited by Weymann at the 1964 Commercial Motor Show. These were the company's last new double-deckers; subsequent new buses were AEC Reliances and Bristol REs. Five Lolines were delivered to Luton Corporation in 1965. These had bodies built by Neepsend, the East Lancs associate company, and, like previous Lolines, were Leyland-engined. As at Aldershot & District they were the operator's last double-deckers, subsequent purchases being one-man-operated Bristol single-deckers.

West Wales of Tycroes bought one Willowbrook-bodied Renown in 1963, following the sale of its Wulfrunian to West Riding, while in Scotland Smith of Barrhead bought a pair with Park Royal bodies, joining the company's two 1961 Bridgemasters. And one Renown, also bodied by Park Royal, joined the Scottish Omnibuses fleet. It was a replacement for a Bridgemaster which had been ordered by Baxter's of Airdrie, giving AEC the chance to demonstrate the virtues of the Bridgemaster's successor to Scotland's biggest AEC operator, which was running around 500 Reliances, Monocoaches, Regals and

BELOW: The other Baxter's Bridgemaster was delivered to Scottish Omnibuses, which had taken over the Baxter's business at the end of 1962. This view in Edinburgh was recorded in 1966, by which time the bus had been fitted with a standard Scottish Bus Group destination display and repainted from its original light green to the dark green adopted by Scottish Omnibuses in 1965. Harry Hay

Regents. The only other Scottish Renowns were two for A1 Service of Ardrossan in 1964, also bodied by Park Royal. And the only others for independents, also in 1964, were one for Red Rover and two for King Alfred – both of which had previously bought new Bridgemasters. The King Alfred vehicles were unusual in being 3B2RA models with semi-automatic gearboxes.

East Yorkshire, with 50 Bridgemasters delivered in the years 1960-3, took its first Renowns in 1964 – 10, with Park Royal bodies. A further 24 followed over the next two years. Western Welsh, another Bridgemaster-operating BET subsidiary, took 15 Renowns in the winter of 1964/5. These had 67-seat Northern Counties bodies – the first on Renown chassis. Another 13 identical buses were delivered in 1965/6.

Two Leyland-oriented BET fleets joined the short list of Lowlander customers in 1964. Yorkshire Woollen took 14 with 72-seat Weymann bodies, but more interesting were 10 of the relatively uncommon LR3 model for Ribble, a company which had been buying lowbridge Atlanteans for routes with height restrictions. They had Alexander bodies with full-width fronts, continuing a practice established by Ribble when it bought its first forward-entrance Titans in 1958. The full-fronted Titans had a smooth front profile and looked acceptable, but the bulbous front cowl designed for the Lowlanders appeared a bit odd. Ribble took six

more in 1965 – and in 1967 acquired the original Lowlander demonstrator when it took over the business of Bamber Bridge Motor Services. Ribble rebuilt its Alexander body with a later style of front dome to make space for the company's standard destination display.

By this time the Wulfrunian was on the way out. West Riding had persevered, taking 25 in 1963 and a further 30 in 1965; a final order for 25 was cancelled. And that was the end for the Wulfrunian. Total production was 137, of which 126 were for West Riding. Besides two demonstrators there were two buses each for Accrington, Wolverhampton and County Motors and one each for Bury, LUT and West Wales.

The end was also in sight for the Lowlander and the Renown. In the autumn of 1965 Leyland – which had taken control of AEC in 1962 – announced that it would be taking no more orders for either model. Neither model was selling well, and Leyland had just taken a shareholding in Bristol – a move which gave the state-owned business access to the open market rather than being confined to supplying state-owned bus operators. So anyone wanting a low-height bus could now buy a Lodekka with, for Lowlander operators, the option of a Leyland engine.

Among municipal AEC operators Rotherham had received three Roe-bodied Renowns in 1964; although built in Leeds, the Roe bodies were to the standard Park Royal design, apart from having the emergency exit on the offside of the body, behind the rear axle, rather than on the rear of the bus. Leicester, which, like Rotherham, was operating a small number of Bridgemasters, added three Renowns to its fleet in 1965. These had full-height East Lancs bodies and were Leicester's only forward-entrance half-cab double-deckers. A further ten East Lancs-bodied Renowns in 1966

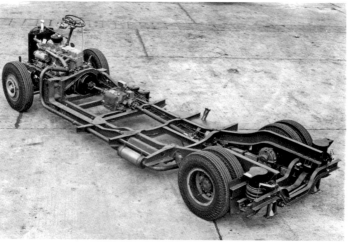

LEFT: This photograph, dated June 1962, is of the first Renown chassis, one month before its launch. It shows how the engine is canted towards the nearside, as well as the location of the semi-automatic gearbox, the air suspension on the rear axle, and the complex frame required to provide a low forward entrance. AEC

were more unusual in being full-height and having rear entrances. The only other rear-entrance Renowns were in the Leigh Corporation fleet.

More interesting was the biggest single order for Renowns – 35 for Nottingham City Transport in 1965. These had full-height 70-seat Weymann bodies and were specified to take advantage of the improved step-free entrance which was possible with a low-height chassis. They entered service in the first half of the year and were followed at the end of the year by seven more with Northern Counties bodies. Five Nottingham-style buses, but with bodies completed by Metro-Cammell following the closure of the associated Weymann business, were purchased by Wolverhampton Corporation in 1966 and were the operator's first-ever AECs.

The small West Bridgford Urban District Council fleet had standardised on AEC Regents. Most had highbridge bodies, but lowbridge vehicles were required for a route to Clifton. So when two lowbridge buses had to be replaced in 1965 West

Bridgford bought a pair of Renowns. These had 74-seat East Lancs bodies and were the first 30ft-long buses in the West Bridgford fleet. They were also the operator's last new double-deckers; its next purchases, in 1967, would be AEC Swifts. Nottingham City Transport took over the West Bridgford operation in 1968.

The Wolverhampton and West Bridgford buses had Monocontrol transmissions and took to just ten the number of Renowns so fitted. All of the others had synchromesh gearboxes.

Having taken its first Renowns in 1963, City of Oxford then standardised on the model, adding short Park Royal-bodied examples each year from 1964 to 1966. Its last Renowns, a batch of four in 1967, were the last to be built, but unlike previous deliveries they had Northern Counties bodies.

In all 251 Renowns were built, and, as with the Bridgemaster, BET was a major buyer, taking 157 for five of its subsidiaries – City of Oxford, East Yorkshire, North Western, South Wales and Western

BELOW LEFT AND RIGHT: A Renown demonstrator was painted in London Transport Country Area dark green, operating for a short period from LT's Northfleet garage; it was then sold to Osborne of Tollesbury, in whose service it is seen in Colchester (left). Eventually it was purchased for preservation and restored to LT green, with the addition of London Transport fleetnames (which it had not originally carried), as seen at a rally in 1981 (right). Stewart J. Brown, Tony Wilson

ABOVE: This AEC Renown demonstrator of 1963 is seen in 1965 operating on hire to Edinburgh Corporation, where it was trialled alongside two other demonstrators, a Fleetline from Daimler and an Atlantean from Leyland. Edinburgh at this time had a predominantly Leyland fleet. The Renown didn't stand much chance against the new generation of rear-engined buses, its only plus-point perhaps being fuel economy of 8.56mpg, although even that wasn't significantly better than the 8.25 of the Fleetline or the 8.2 of the Atlantean.
Harry Hay

Welsh. Apart from North Western all had previously bought Bridgemasters. Park Royal bodywork was fitted to 133 Renowns; the other builders which bodied the type were East Lancs (33), Northern Counties (39), Metro-Cammell/Weymann (40) and Willowbrook (six).

The last Scottish Lowlanders were delivered to Western SMT in 1965. There were six, all bodied by Northern Counties. Five were on new chassis, but the sixth was on the chassis which had been built in 1962 and supplied to, but not used by, Edinburgh Corporation. Western's 1965 Lowlanders were the company's last new half-cabs and were accompanied by 54 Alexander-bodied Daimler Fleetlines – a clear illustration of how the bus industry was changing.

The only Lowlanders registered in 1966 were a single Northern Counties-bodied example for South Notts and a batch of four for East Midland with Metro-Cammell bodies to the same design as those built by Weymann for Yorkshire Woollen two years earlier. The very last Lowlander, for South Notts, entered service in 1967.

Lowlander production amounted to 274 chassis, of which 192 – 70% – went to Scottish Bus Group companies. Leyland's new approach to low-height buses was a modified version of the Atlantean, the PDR1/2, which used the Lowlander's drop-centre rear axle. It entered production in 1964. Many buyers, among them Manchester and Nottingham, specified the PDR1/2 for its step-free lower-saloon gangway rather than because it could be bodied to a low overall height. One of the first buyers of PDR1/2s with low-height bodywork was West Riding, in 1966, when it finally gave up on the Wulfrunian.

The last Lolines were five with Northern Counties bodies for Halifax Joint Omnibus Committee in 1967. These had Gardner 6LX engines, five-speed SCG semi-automatic gearboxes (thought to be the first five-speed semi-automatics in a British double-deck bus) and Bristol rear axles. At this point Dennis made its exit from the bus business.

One of the Halifax buses was used for a road test by *Bus & Coach* magazine. It was part-loaded, and returned fuel consumption of 12mpg overall and 8.65mpg with four stops per mile. Its maximum speed was 57mph, at a time when the legal limit for buses and coaches was 50mph except on motorways, where there was no limit.

The five Lolines supplied to Halifax had short lives with their original owner, being sold in 1970 to West Riding, which was buying vast numbers of second-hand buses – mainly Lodekkas – to replace its Wulfrunians. By this time West Riding was a National Bus Company subsidiary. The last of West Riding's Wulfrunians were withdrawn in 1972, by which time the survivors had been downseated from 75 to 67 by the removal of eight seats at the front of the upper deck, to reduce the load on the front suspension.

Loline production (excluding the unbodied prototype) totalled 280 – 48 of the original model, 48 of the Mk II and 184 of the Mk III. BET companies took 196, of which 141 – 50% of total Loline production – were for Aldershot & District. No Lolines were sold new in Scotland or Wales, but one did go to Northern Ireland, and another was exported to Hong Kong.

Thus 1967 marked the end of the Lodekka competitors, 11 low-height buses entering service with E-suffix registrations – one Lowlander for South Notts, five Lolines for Halifax, one Renown for Leigh and four Renowns for City of Oxford. The Lodekka itself continued in production until 1968, the last G-registered buses entering service with Midland General in September.

The low-height chassis from AEC and Leyland were competing with each manufacturer's standard double-deck models, the Regent V and Titan respectively. The standard chassis were simpler, cheaper, and of proven reliability. A comment by South Wales Transport General Manager H. Weedy, in the September 1962 issue of the *AEC Gazette*, makes the point about cost in a comparison between the Regent V and the Renown: 'Whilst the [Regent] Mk V chassis has been most satisfactory in service, the new Renown has the edge by virtue of its low frame height and excellent suspension characteristics. The only factor which restricts its immediate adoption as a fleet chassis is the higher cost of the refinements which contribute to its superiority.'

Only Dennis did not have a conventional chassis, so all Loline sales represented extra business for the company.

Sales of mainstream low-height chassis (i.e. excluding the Wulfrunian) were as follows:

Loline	280
Lowlander	274
Renown	251
Bridgemaster	180

The best year for deliveries of each type was:

Bridgemaster	50 in 1961
Loline	70 in 1962
Lowlander	199 in 1963
Renown	94 in 1965

The 199 Lowlanders delivered in 1963 represented just under three-quarters of all Lowlander sales, the figure being inflated by late deliveries of vehicles which should have entered service with the Scottish Bus Group in the previous year. And more than half of the 1965 Renowns were for one customer, Nottingham City Transport, which bought the model for its low floor, not for its low height. Surprisingly, AEC actually delivered more Renowns than Regent Vs to UK fleets in 1965.

The availability of low-floor chassis obviously contributed to the demise of lowbridge side-gangway bodywork. After the launch of the Bridgemaster AEC sold just over 50 Regent Vs with lowbridge bodywork, the last of these going to Bedwas & Machen Urban District Council in 1964. Similarly the Lowlander virtually brought to an end the lowbridge Titan. The last for an English operator was delivered to South Notts in 1962, following which the company switched to the Lowlander. Small numbers of Titans with Massey lowbridge bodies were bought by municipal fleets in South Wales, the last, a PD3, going to Bedwas & Machen in 1968. It was the last lowbridge bus built.

There were other factors influencing attitudes towards low-height double-deckers. A typical lowbridge bus of the 1940s was 26ft long and seated 53 people. If at the end of a nominal 15-year life it was going to be replaced by an early-1960s low-height double-decker, its replacement would be 30ft long and seat around 70. But bus use was in decline; from a peak of 13,000,000,000 journeys per year at the start of the 1950s it had dropped 20%, to just under 10,500,000,000, by the mid-1960s. The move to bigger buses was

allowing operators to run fewer buses on timetables with wider headways. However, if what was wanted was a straightforward like-for-like 53-seat replacement, for example on a service running every 30 minutes where the frequency could not easily be reduced, the answer in the early 1960s was to replace a time-expired 53-seat double-decker with a new 36ft-long 53-seat single-decker.

The availability of high-capacity single-deckers provided a practical – and less expensive – alternative to buying a low-height double-decker (or, indeed, any type of double-decker). Thus instead of replacing a lowbridge Regent III with a new Renown there was the option of replacing it with a 36ft Reliance, the major drawback for urban operation being the Reliance's three-step entrance. To improve accessibility some operators went for low-frame rear-engined single-deckers – but then found that, generally, the promise of high capacity and ease of boarding was nullified by the reality of in-service unreliability.

Most low-height buses enjoyed normal operating lives, typically 12 or 15 years, depending on the operator. These figures were fixed in part by the system of vehicle certification in force at the time. Typically a new bus was given a seven-year Certificate of Fitness, and following a major overhaul it would generally be recertified for another five years' use; another overhaul would normally obtain a three-year CoF, and after that most operators either withdrew the vehicle or carried out such remedial work as was necessary to obtain a further CoF, which might be valid for only one year.

ABOVE: The blue Renown demonstrator was purchased by Burwell & District, being seen here in Cambridge in the autumn of 1965. It ran for Burwell & District until 1977. Geoff Mills

ABOVE: The first AEC Renowns to enter service joined the South Wales Transport fleet in the spring of 1963 and had 71-seat Park Royal bodies. There were 14, and they followed 22 Bridgemasters bought new, plus one ex-demonstrator. The Park Royal body for the Renown looked less top-heavy than that for the Bridgemaster, with greater curvature on the front and rear domes. It also had the entrance against the bulkhead, unlike that on forward-entrance Bridgemasters. Reg Wilson

BELOW: Along with the Park Royal-bodied Renowns South Wales Transport took five with 71-seat Willowbrook bodies, which were delivered towards the end of 1963. Geoffrey Morant

ABOVE: The only other Renown to be bodied by Willowbrook also went to Wales, being supplied to independent West Wales of Tycroes, where it replaced a short-lived Wulfrunian. It was new in 1963. Geoffrey Morant

BELOW: North Western switched from Dennis Lolines in 1962 to AEC Renowns in 1963; one of each stands in the parking area at Blackpool's Coliseum bus station. There were 18 Renowns in the company's 1963 order, and these would be followed by 15 in 1964, all with Park Royal bodies. AEC must have been pleased to win double-deck business from North Western, as it had hitherto been supplying only Reliance single-deck chassis. In between these two orders North Western also took 20 Alexander-bodied Fleetlines, and it was the Fleetline which would become the company's standard double-decker. The advert on the side of the Renown is for a car dealer selling long-vanished makes Hillman, Humber, Singer and Sunbeam – all part of the Rootes group of companies. Roy Marshall

ABOVE: City of Oxford followed its Bridgemasters with Renowns, with the first being ten short Park Royal-bodied 65-seaters in 1963. This early-1970s view shows the simplified livery adopted in 1970, which used just two colours rather than three. Geoffrey Morant

BELOW: After buying rear-entrance Loline IIIs Leigh Corporation took delivery four AEC Renowns with rear-entrance East Lancs bodies at the end of 1963. Leigh would standardise on the Renown, buying another 14 between 1964 and 1966, but with forward-entrance bodies. Only Leigh and Leicester specified rear-entrance bodywork on Renown chassis. Geoffrey Morant

LEFT: This 1964 bus, with its forward-entrance East Lancs body, is typical of Leigh's later Renowns. 'Beachcomber' seems a somewhat fanciful name for a coffee bar in landlocked Warrington. Roy Marshall

RIGHT: Reading joined the small number of municipal Loline buyers in 1962 and by 1966 was running 26, with attractive East Lancs bodies. This is a 1973 view of one of the 1962 buses, with a Bristol RE in the background. A. E. Jones

LEFT: A new bodybuilder appeared on the Loline in 1964, Aldershot & District having ordered 50 with bodywork by Weymann of Addlestone. They were the company's last new double-deckers and took its Loline fleet to 141, which was almost three times greater than the next-biggest fleet of 50 at North Western. John May

ABOVE LEFT AND RIGHT: The sole Park Royal-bodied AEC Renown for Scottish Omnibuses is pictured outside the AEC factory in Southall before delivery at the end of 1963. It was supplied in place of a Bridgemaster which had been ordered by Baxter's of Airdrie. AEC

BELOW: After two further Bridgemasters in 1961 the next new double-deckers for King Alfred Motor Services were two Renowns with Park Royal bodies in 1964. The rearward-sliding externally mounted cab door was an unusual feature. In 1967 King Alfred reverted to Leyland double-deckers, taking four PDR1/2 Atlanteans. John May

ABOVE: Scotland's last new Renowns were a pair of Park Royal-bodied buses delivered to a member of the A1 Service co-operative, McKinnon of Kilmarnock. They both operated for 15 years with A1. This one is seen when new. Harry Hay

BELOW: Red Rover of Aylesbury, which was already running two Bridgemasters, bought a Park Royal-bodied Renown in 1964. It was the company's last new double-decker. Roy Marshall

LEFT: From 1964 to 1966 Western Welsh bought Renowns with Northern Counties bodies, building up a fleet of 28. They were 28ft-long 67-seaters.

RIGHT: In 1964 Yorkshire Woollen added 14 Lowlanders to its fleet. They had 72-seat Weymann bodies which were to a quite different design from Weymann's body for the Dennis Loline. This was in contrast to Alexander, which used the same basic body design for both chassis. Geoffrey Morant

LEFT: An unusual adaptation of its standard Lowlander body to incorporate a full-width cab was developed by Alexander for two batches of buses supplied to Ribble in 1964/5. The aim was to provide some visual commonality with Ribble's huge fleet of full-front PD3s, although the end result was not particularly attractive. A nearside cab door gave access to the engine bay. This bus is seen in Fleetwood in 1969. A. E. Jones

LEFT: The low-floor benefit of the Renown clearly appealed in the Midlands. Following Leicester and Nottingham, Wolverhampton took five full-height Renowns in 1966 with Metro-Cammell bodies completed on frames supplied by Weymann, to the same design as the buses supplied to Nottingham in 1965, with their distinctive deep windows. Roy Marshall

RIGHT: In the mid-1960s West Bridgford Urban District Council ran just 28 buses – 25 AEC Regents and three Daimlers, which were AEC-powered CWA6s. Two Renowns with 74-seat East Lancs bodies joined the fleet in 1965. They were the undertaking's last double-deckers. Roy Marshall

LEFT: The West Bridgford bus operation was absorbed by neighbouring Nottingham City Transport in 1968. The Renowns soon received Nottingham livery and had the brightwork stripped from the radiator grille – an act of municipal vandalism which was inflicted on all of Nottingham's Renowns. Roy Marshall

LEFT: In 1966 East Yorkshire added ten Park Royal-bodied Renowns to its fleet. They were the company's last new AEC double-deckers. East Yorkshire ran 84 low-height AECs – 34 Renowns and 50 Bridgemasters.
Geoffrey Morant

RIGHT: City of Oxford standardised on short Renowns with Park Royal bodies until delivery of its last five, in 1967, which were instead bodied by Northern Counties. Similar to buses supplied to Western Welsh in 1965/6, they were the last Renowns built. One is seen bearing NBC's corporate Oxford South Midland fleetname in the early 1970s.
Roy Marshall

LEFT: The last new low-height front-engined double-deckers came from Dennis, with the delivery of five Loline IIIs to Halifax in 1967. They were bodied by Northern Counties. Here one nears the summit of the long climb from Elland on its way from Halifax to Huddersfield. Arthur Wilson via Don Akrigg

ABOVE: The Lodekka was far and away the most successful of the low-height models of the 1950s and 1960s. Towards the end of production output was focussed on the 30ft-long forward-entrance FLF model. This is a 1963 FLF6G in service with Eastern National in Clacton-on-Sea in 1978, looking well for a 15-year-old bus nearing the end of its life. Stewart J. Brown

LEFT: Low-height buses made side-gangway lowbridge models obsolete, but it took a long time for the lowbridge bus to disappear. This was the last to be built – a Massey-bodied Leyland Titan PD3 delivered to Bedwas & Machen in 1968. It seems ironic that this lowbridge PD3 should have been delivered after the final examples of the Lowlander, which had been developed to replace it. Stewart J. Brown

Chapter Four

IN LATER LIFE

ABOVE: Yorkshire Woollen, which was operating Leyland Lowlanders, acquired eight Bridgemasters from South Wales Transport in 1969, making it one of the few operators to run both Lowlanders and Bridgemasters. Geoffrey Morant

ABOVE: United Counties acquired both Lolines and Lowlanders when it took over Luton's municipal bus operation in 1970. This is a 1965 Loline III with East Lancs body, seen in United Counties' colours in 1973. A. E. Jones

The National Bus Company was created in 1969 to unite the businesses previously controlled by the Transport Holding Company and the BET group, and it operated examples of all types of low-height buses. It acquired Bridgemasters, Renowns, Lolines and Lowlanders from a range of BET subsidiaries. It also briefly operated Wulfrunians at West Riding but soon started replacing them with Lodekkas from other fleets. The five Halifax Lolines were bought by West Riding in 1970. NBC acquired eight Lolines and 16 Lowlanders when United Counties bought the Luton Corporation bus operation in 1970. It also collected King Alfred's Bridgemasters and Renowns when that business was bought by Hants & Dorset in 1973.

There were some changes of operators of NBC's low-height buses in the late 1960s and early 1970s. Almost 120 Lolines were still running for Aldershot & District when it was merged with former THC subsidiary Thames Valley in 1971 to create the new Alder Valley company. Former THC business Crosville acquired 16 AEC Renowns and 11 Dennis Lolines when the North Western business was broken up in January 1972; at this time all of Crosville's double-deckers were Bristol Lodekkas. Yorkshire Woollen, which was

short of vehicles, received eight Bridgemasters from South Wales in 1969.

In Scotland, all of the Lowlanders operated by Central SMT and a number of those at Western SMT were soon redistributed to other fleets. All 30 of Central's were transferred in 1965 to Fife and Highland. Western followed Central's example and disposed of 32 Lowlanders in 1966/7, Fife and Highland again being the recipients.

A few low-height buses saw service with the Passenger Transport Executives which were created in 1969/70 and 1974. SELNEC, serving Manchester and its hinterland, acquired Lolines and Renowns from one of its original constituents, Leigh. More examples of both followed in 1972 with the acquisition from NBC of part of the North Western Road Car Co, bringing with it 39 Lolines and 17 Renowns. There were two ex-Luton Lowlanders in the fleet of Godfrey Abbot, which was purchased by Greater Manchester in 1976, making them (briefly) the only PTE owned Lowlanders. At nearby Merseyside there was just one low-height bus in the PTE fleet, the former Bridgemaster demonstrator operated by Liverpool Corporation. West Midlands gained Renowns from Wolverhampton and Lolines from Walsall; it was also heir to Wolverhampton's two Wulfrunians, which were withdrawn without receiving PTE livery. And South Yorkshire inherited, from Rotherham, three out-of-service Renowns which were immediately sold, even though they were only nine years old.

Comparatively few low-height double-deckers found new lives with smaller operators when they were withdrawn by their original owners. There were a number of reasons for this. The bus industry's operating costs were rising, and there were widespread difficulties in recruiting drivers and conductors. The Government was also encouraging the switch to one-man operation by providing a 50% grant towards the price of new buses for use on regular service. All of this depressed demand for second-hand double-deckers as many small operators which in the 1960s had acquired second-hand Titans and Regents took advantage of the Government's largesse and instead bought new Bedfords and Fords which could be run without a conductor. So in the 1970s ageing double-deckers tended to be scrapped or to be bought for use on contract services where the Government grant was not available, as was the case with Bedlington & District, which bought 24 Renowns from City of Oxford, and Newton of Dingwall, which managed to become Scotland's biggest Bridgemaster operator by acquiring five ex-Cardiff examples.

Notable among independent purchases was the acquisition in 1968 of two former Smith of Barrhead Renowns by Barton Transport (an operator which in the 1970s would take full advantage of New Bus Grant to renew its fleet with modern coaches); the Smith bus operation had been acquired by Western SMT, which did not want the non-standard vehicles. Surprisingly a few Guy Wulfrunians found short lives with second operators, this select group including one West Riding bus which became Scotland's only Wulfrunian, running for a short time for McLennan of Spittalfield. Bury's sole example headed to Wales, where it was operated by Howells & Withers of Pontllanfraith in South Wales before passing to Wright's of Wrexham and then back to England with Berresford's of Cheddleton, a repository for odd buses in the 1960s and 1970s.

By the time these low-height double-deckers were being withdrawn there was a bus-preservation movement in Britain – not as strong as that we know now, but with enough hard-working

ABOVE: Under NBC ownership there was a rapid clear-out of West Riding's troublesome Wulfrunians. Most of the replacements were Bristol Lodekkas, but among the more unusual purchases were Halifax's five Lolines, which were just three years old. They were acquired before NBC adopted a corporate identity and were thus repainted in West Riding green, although by the time of the photograph this bus had gained NBC advertising, and its wheels were in corporate NBC grey. John May

supporters to ensure the survival of examples of all of the types covered in this book. Thus there are, for example, Lolines from Aldershot & District, City of Oxford and Middlesbrough, Renowns from King Alfred, Western Welsh, Leicester and Nottingham, a Western SMT Lowlander, Liverpool, Leicester and City of Oxford Bridgemasters and even a West Riding Wulfrunian.

And, despite their limited sales, examples of the Renown, Loline and Lowlander would be the subject of 1:76 die-cast scale models. From specialist manufacturer Britbus came the Alexander-bodied Loline, which first appeared in 2005 and was followed by the Alexander-bodied Lowlander in 2007. EFE modelled the Park Royal-bodied AEC Renown. All three models have been produced in the liveries of the main operators of each type.

RIGHT: Two Passenger Transport Executives – SELNEC and West Midlands – inherited AEC Renowns from their constituent municipalities. Those at SELNEC came from Leigh and had East Lancs bodies. This is a 1972 view. Geoff Mills

LEFT: Crosville took over part of the business of former BET company North Western in 1972, acquiring AEC Renowns, Dennis Lolines and Daimler Fleetlines in the process. A freshly repainted Renown is seen at Nantwich depot in April 1972; other ex-North Western buses are visible inside the garage building on the left.
A. E. Jones

RIGHT: Some of North Western's Renowns were taken over by SELNEC PTE when it absorbed the company's operations in the PTE's area. This is a 1976 view in Manchester, by which time SELNEC had become Greater Manchester.
Stewart J. Brown

LEFT: NBC's Alder Valley subsidiary, created in January 1972 by the merger of the ex-BET Aldershot & District and ex-THC Thames Valley companies, initially adopted a livery of deep red, as seen on the Weymann-bodied Loline nearer the camera. The bus alongside is in NBC poppy red.
Stewart J. Brown

LEFT: By 1975 this Alder Valley Loline III had been demoted to driver-training duties, despite being just 13 years old. Provision has been made for a trainer to sit behind the trainee driver, and a standard-sized side window has replaced the solid metal panel where the staircase would once have been. It has an Alexander body and is seen in **Reading.** Tony Wilson

ABOVE: In the mid-1970s Alder Valley suffered a severe shortage of vehicles, which saw it hiring in buses from other NBC subsidiaries and from some unlikely outside sources, including Southend Transport, which in the summer of 1974 supplied this Alexander-bodied Albion Lowlander. It had been converted for one-man operation by Southend; the panel below the route number could be illuminated to warn passengers to pay the driver. Southend even tried to improve passenger flow by painting the words 'Entrance' and 'Exit' on the entry step, although one wonders how many passengers would have noticed. Stewart J. Brown collection

LEFT: Under NBC's corporate identity programme it was briefly intended that East Yorkshire buses should be blue, but that decision was quickly changed, and they were instead repainted red. This is a 1963 bus, from the final batch of Bridgemasters built, trying to convince passers by in Hull that it's best by bus. East Yorkshire's were the only Bridgemasters to receive NBC poppy red. Geoffrey Morant

RIGHT: City of Oxford's buses were also painted poppy red, replacing the company's unusual and distinctive red and pale green. This is a 1963 Renown. Roy Marshall

BELOW LEFT AND RIGHT: East Midland's buses had been dark red but adopted leaf green in the NBC era. The new look is shown on a 1963 Alexander-bodied Lowlander (top) and on a 1966 bus with Metro-Cammell body. The newer vehicle was similar to the Weymann-bodied buses that had been delivered two years earlier to Yorkshire Woollen, even down to the same three-section destination display. David Powell, Stewart J. Brown collection

ABOVE: While most NBC buses were either poppy red or leaf green, some of those operated by Northern General group companies in the area served by Tyneside Passenger Transport Executive received PTE yellow livery – albeit applied in corporate NBC style, as seen on this ex-East Yorkshire Renown in the Tyneside Omnibus Co fleet in Newcastle in 1973. Stewart J. Brown

BELOW: Central SMT withdrew all 30 of its Lowlanders after just three years in service. They were transferred to sister SBG companies Alexander (Fife) and Highland. Here a Northern Counties-bodied bus in Kirkcaldy operates a colliery service for Alexander (Fife). Stewart J. Brown

LEFT: Highland Omnibuses double-deckers in the early 1960s were maroon with one or two bands of cream relief. The arrival of its first Central SMT Lowlanders in 1965 saw the company adopt Central's livery, which used a similar shade of red but with cream window surrounds. Thus the ex Central buses were not immediately repainted, while those acquired from Western were given the Central-style livery, as seen on this bus in Inverness in 1973. The Lowlander in the background is another ex-Central bus, in Highland's new colours of poppy red and peacock blue, introduced in 1972. Both buses have Northern Counties bodywork. Stewart J. Brown

RIGHT: Competing approaches to low-height design in the Highland Omnibuses fleet. In the centre of the picture is the first Albion Lowlander, which had originally operated for Western SMT, as illustrated on page 44. It is flanked by two AEC Bridgemasters, transferred to Highland from Scottish Omnibuses. The bus on the left had been the last new double-decker delivered to Baxter's of Airdrie, while that on the right had been ordered by Baxter's but was delivered new to Scottish Omnibuses. Harry Hay

LEFT: The only PTE-owned Lowlanders were two in the fleet of Godfrey Abbot of Sale, Cheshire, which was purchased by Greater Manchester PTE. These ex-United Counties buses had been new to Luton Corporation and were quickly sold by Godfrey Abbot's new owner. In this 1977 view the bus in Godfrey Abbot Group livery is in fact in the fleet of Silver Fox Coaches of Glasgow, making it one of the few Leyland-badged Lowlanders to run in Scotland. New in 1963, it has an East Lancs body. Stewart J. Brown

ABOVE: Red Rover of Aylesbury had bought two new Bridgemasters and one new Renown. It later added this second-hand Renown, one of the ungainly full-height buses purchased by Nottingham City Transport in 1965. Stewart J. Brown

ABOVE: No Lolines were bought new by operators in Scotland, but a few used examples found their way north in the mid 1970s, generally for contract work. Buyers included Allander Coaches of Milngavie and, as seen here, Wilson of Carnwath, with an ex-Alder Valley Loline III with Alexander body. This is a 1977 view at the operator's depot, with the bus apparently experiencing some battery trouble. Stewart J. Brown

RIGHT: The move to one-man operation in the 1970s, supported by a Government subsidy for buyers of new buses, meant that when they were withdrawn by their original owners relatively few low-height buses saw further service with independents other than on contracts. There were exceptions, and in 1973 this 12-year-old Loline was running for Norfolk's of Nayland on its service to Colchester. Norfolk's livery was green, and the former Aldershot & District bus fitted into its new owner's fleet without the need for a repaint. Stewart J. Brown

LEFT: One contract operator which bought second-hand AEC Renowns was Bedlington & District Coaches of Ashington. They were used primarily for colliery services. The company had 20 ex-Nottingham Renowns, purchased in 1977, and these ran in Nottingham livery with the addition of BDC logos on the side. There were also a few ex-Oxford and ex-Rotherham Renowns in the fleet. Stewart J. Brown collection

ABOVE: One of Leigh's 14 forward-entrance East Lancs-bodied AEC Renowns is among those low-height buses that have survived in preservation. A 72-seater new in 1965, it is normally housed at the Museum of Transport in Manchester. Stewart J. Brown

RIGHT: The Scottish Omnibuses AEC Renown illustrated on page 59 is one of the many low-height buses available in 1:76 scale. It is an **EFE model.** Stewart J. Brown

ABOVE: Alexander-bodied Albion Lowlanders and Dennis Lolines are produced by Britbus. This is an ex-North Western Loline in Crosville livery. Gordon Ferguson

BELOW: The end. An Alexander (Midland) Lowlander leaving Glasgow's Buchanan Bus Station shows the neat rear-end arrangement of Alexander's low-height body, as fitted to both Lowlanders and Lolines. Stewart J. Brown collection

Appendices

I. Deliveries

AEC Bridgemaster

	1956	1957	1958	1959	1960	1961	1962	1963	Total
AEC demonstrators	1	2	1	1	1				6
Walsall Corporation	1								1
Belfast Corporation			1						1
Sheffield Transport					6	1			7
Western Welsh			13	7					20
South Wales				9	5	8			22
Grimsby-Cleethorpes Transport				2	4				6
King Alfred, Winchester				2		2			4
Southend Corporation				2	4				6
Leicester Corporation				2		5	3		10
Cardiff Corporation				6					6
East Yorkshire					4	16	15	15	50
Red Rover, Aylesbury							1	1	2
Lincoln Corporation							4		4
Rotherham Corporation						5			5
City of Oxford						10	2	11	23
Baxter, Airdrie						1			1
Smith, Barrhead						2			2
East Kent							3		3
Scottish Omnibuses								1	1
Total	2	2	15	31	24	50	28	28	180

In black – B3RA (rear entrance)
In red – 2B3RA (forward entrance)

AEC Renown

	1962	1963	1964	1965	1966	1967	Total
AEC demonstrators	2						2
South Wales		19					19
Leigh Corporation		4	5	4	4	1	18
Scottish Omnibuses		1					1
Smith, Barrhead		2					2
North Western		18	15				33
City of Oxford		10	9	12	8	4	43
West Wales, Tycroes		1					1
East Yorkshire			10	14	10		34
Western Welsh			1	17	10		28
King Alfred, Winchester			2				2
Rotherham Corporation			3				3
Red Rover, Aylesbury			1				1
A1 Service, Ardrossan			2				2
Leicester Corporation				3	10		13
Nottingham City Transport				42			42
West Bridgford UDC				2			2
Wolverhampton Corporation					5		5
Total	2	55	48	94	47	5	251

Dennis Loline

	1957	1958	1959	1960	1961	1962	1963	1964	1965	1966	1967	Total
Blue Bus, Willington	1	1										2
Aldershot & District		34			9	48		22	28			141
Hutchings & Cornelius		1										1
Leigh Corporation		2	2		2							6
Middlesbrough Corporation		1		8								9
Lancashire United			2	4								6
Walsall Corporation		1		16								17
North Western				15	15	20						50
Luton Corporation				2					6			8
Barton Transport				1								1
Belfast Corporation					1							1
China Motor Bus					1							1
City of Oxford				5								5
Dennis demonstrator						1						1

	1957	1958	1959	1960	1961	1962	1963	1964	1965	1966	1967	Total
Reading Corporation						8		10		8		26
Halifax JOC											5	5
Total	1	40	4	46	33	77	-	32	34	8	5	280

In blue – Loline
In red – Loline II
In black – Loline III

Guy Wulfrunian

	1959	1960	1961	1962	1963	1964	1965	Total
West Riding	1	6	44	10	35		30	126
Guy demonstrators		2						2
Lancashire United			1					1
Bury Corporation			1					1
Wolverhampton Corporation				1	1			2
West Wales, Tycroes				1				1
County Motors				2				2
Accrington Corporation				2				2
Total	1	10	50	11	35	-	30	137

Albion Lowlander

	1961	1962	1963	1964	1965	1966	1967	Total
Albion demonstrator	1							1
Western SMT	1	8	89	7	6			111
Central SMT		10	20					30
East Midland		1	13			4		18
Alexander (Fife)			7					7
Alexander (Midland)			41	3				44
Alexander (Northern)			2					2
Luton Corporation			16					16
Southend Corporation			10					10
South Notts, Gotham			1	1	1	1	1	5
Ribble				10	6			16
Yorkshire Woollen				14				14
Total	2	19	199	35	13	5	1	274

Comparative totals

	1956	1957	1958	1959	1960	1961	1962	1963	1964	1965	1966	1967	Total
Bridgemaster	2	2	15	31	24	50	28	28					180
Wulfrunian				1	10	50	11	35	-	30			137
Loline		1	40	4	46	33	77	-	32	34	8	5	280
Lowlander						2	19	199	35	13	5	1	274
Renown							2	55	48	94	47	5	251
Total	2	3	55	36	80	135	137	317	115	171	60	11	1,122

II. Demonstrators

	Registration	New	Bodywork	Disposal
AEC Bridgemaster	9 JML	1956	Crossley H41/31R	Birmingham City Transport
	60 MMD	1957	Crossley H41/31R	South Wales Transport
	76 MME	1957	Crossley H41/31R	Barton Transport
	116 TMD	1958	Park Royal H45/31R	Liverpool Corporation
	80 WMH	1959	Park Royal H45/31R	Osborne, Tollesbury
	2211 MK	1960	Park Royal H43/29F	Osborne, Tollesbury
AEC Renown	7552 MX	1962	Park Royal H39/32F	Burwell & District
	8071 ML	1962	Park Royal H44/31F	Osborne, Tollesbury
Albion Lowlander	747 EUS	1962	Alexander H41/31F	Bamber Bridge Motor Services
Dennis Loline	EPG 179B	1962	Northern Counties H44/32F	Warner's, Tewkesbury
Guy Wulfrunian	7800 DA	1960	Roe H45/33F	West Riding (for spares)
	8072 DA	1960	Roe H41/31F	West Riding (for spares)

III. Chassis lists

AEC Bridgemaster

Chassis number	First owner	Registration	Body	Layout	New	Notes
MB3RA001	Walsall (825)	YDH 225	Crossley	H41/31R	1956	
MB3RA002	AEC (demonstrator)	9 JML	Crossley	H41/31R	1956	1
B3RA003	AEC (demonstrator)	60 MMD	Crossley	H41/31R	1957	2
B3RA004	AEC (demonstrator)	76 MME	Crossley	H41/31R	1957	3
B3RA005	Belfast (550)	WZ 7484	Harkness	H39/31R	1958	
B3RA006	AEC (demonstrator)	116 TMD	Park Royal	H45/31R	1958	4
B3RA007	Sheffield (519)	2519 WE	Park Royal	H45/31R	1959	
B3RA008	Sheffield (520)	2520 WE	Park Royal	H45/31R	1959	
B3RA009	Sheffield (521)	2521 WE	Park Royal	H45/31R	1959	
B3RA010	Sheffield (522)	2522 WE	Park Royal	H45/31R	1959	
B3RA011	Sheffield (523)	2523 WE	Park Royal	H45/31R	1959	
B3RA012	Sheffield (524)	2524 WE	Park Royal	H45/31R	1959	
B3RA013	Western Welsh (683)	PBO 683	Park Royal	H41/27RD	1958	
B3RA014	Western Welsh (684)	PBO 684	Park Royal	H41/27RD	1958	
B3RA015	Western Welsh (685)	PBO 685	Park Royal	H41/27RD	1958	
B3RA016	Western Welsh (686)	PBO 686	Park Royal	H41/27RD	1958	
B3RA017	Western Welsh (687)	PBO 687	Park Royal	H41/27RD	1958	
B3RA018	Western Welsh (688)	PBO 688	Park Royal	H41/27RD	1958	
B3RA019	Western Welsh (689)	PBO 689	Park Royal	H41/27RD	1958	
B3RA020	Western Welsh (690)	PBO 690	Park Royal	H41/27RD	1958	
B3RA021	Western Welsh (691)	PBO 691	Park Royal	H41/27RD	1958	
B3RA022	Western Welsh (692)	PBO 692	Park Royal	H41/27RD	1958	
B3RA023	Western Welsh (693)	PBO 693	Park Royal	H41/27RD	1958	
B3RA024	Western Welsh (694)	PBO 694	Park Royal	H41/27RD	1958	
B3RA025	Western Welsh (695)	PBO 695	Park Royal	H41/27RD	1958	
B3RA026	Western Welsh (696)	PBO 696	Park Royal	H41/27RD	1959	
B3RA027	Western Welsh (697)	PBO 697	Park Royal	H41/27RD	1959	
B3RA028	Western Welsh (698)	PBO 698	Park Royal	H41/27RD	1959	
B3RA029	Western Welsh (699)	PBO 699	Park Royal	H41/27RD	1959	
B3RA030	Western Welsh (700)	PBO 700	Park Royal	H41/27RD	1959	
B3RA031	Western Welsh (701)	PBO 701	Park Royal	H41/27RD	1959	
B3RA032	Western Welsh (702)	PBO 702	Park Royal	H41/27RD	1959	
B3RA033	South Wales (1199)	RCY 369	Park Royal	H41/31R	1959	
B3RA034	South Wales (1200)	RCY 370	Park Royal	H41/31R	1959	
B3RA035	South Wales (1201)	RCY 371	Park Royal	H41/31R	1959	
B3RA036	South Wales (1202)	RCY 372	Park Royal	H41/31R	1959	
B3RA037	Grimsby-Cleethorpes (108)	MEE 700	Park Royal	H41/27R	1959	
B3RA038	Grimsby-Cleethorpes (109)	MEE 701	Park Royal	H41/27R	1959	
B3RA039	AEC (demonstrator)	80 WMH	Park Royal	H45/31R	1959	5
040	(not built)					
B3RA041	South Wales (1203)	UCY 837	Park Royal	H41/31R	1959	
B3RA042	South Wales (1204)	UCY 838	Park Royal	H41/31R	1959	
B3RA043	South Wales (1205)	UCY 839	Park Royal	H41/31R	1959	
B3RA044	South Wales (1206)	UCY 840	Park Royal	H41/31R	1959	
B3RA045	South Wales (1207)	UCY 841	Park Royal	H41/31R	1959	
B3RA046	King Alfred, Winchester	WCG 106	Park Royal	H45/29R	1959	
B3RA047	King Alfred, Winchester	WCG 107	Park Royal	H45/29R	1959	
B3RA048	Southend (317)	SJN 636	Park Royal	H45/31R	1959	
B3RA049	Southend (318)	SJN 637	Park Royal	H45/31R	1959	
B3RA050	Leicester (213)	VJF 213	Park Royal	H41/31R	1959	
B3RA051	Leicester (214)	VJF 214	Park Royal	H41/31R	1959	
B3RA052	Cardiff (361)	TUH 361	Park Royal	H41/27RD	1960	
B3RA053	Cardiff (362)	TUH 362	Park Royal	H41/27RD	1960	
B3RA054	Cardiff (363)	TUH 363	Park Royal	H41/27RD	1960	
B3RA055	Cardiff (364)	TUH 364	Park Royal	H41/27RD	1960	
B3RA056	Cardiff (365)	TUH 365	Park Royal	H41/27RD	1960	
B3RA057	Cardiff (366)	TUH 366	Park Royal	H41/27RD	1960	
B3RA058	East Yorkshire (696)	6696 KH	Park Royal	H45/31RD	1960	
B3RA059	East Yorkshire (697)	6697 KH	Park Royal	H45/31RD	1960	
B3RA060	East Yorkshire (698)	6698 KH	Park Royal	H45/31RD	1960	
B3RA061	East Yorkshire (699)	6699 KH	Park Royal	H45/31RD	1960	
2B3RA062	South Wales (1208)	WCY 888	Park Royal	H43/29F	1960	
2B3RA063	South Wales (1209)	WCY 889	Park Royal	H43/29F	1960	
2B3RA064	South Wales (1210)	WCY 890	Park Royal	H43/29F	1960	
2B3RA065	South Wales (1211)	WCY 891	Park Royal	H43/29F	1960	
2B3RA066	South Wales (1212)	WCY 892	Park Royal	H43/29F	1960	
2B3RA067	AEC (demonstrator)	2211 MK	Park Royal	H43/29F	1960	6

Chassis number	First owner	Registration	Body	Layout	New	Notes
068	(not built)					
B3RA069	Southend (319)	WHJ 430	Park Royal	H45/31R	1960	
B3RA070	Southend (320)	WHJ 431	Park Royal	H45/31R	1960	
B3RA071	Southend (321)	WHJ 432	Park Royal	H45/31R	1960	
B3RA072	Southend (322)	WHJ 433	Park Royal	H45/31R	1960	
B3RA073	Grimsby-Cleethorpes (130)	NJV 992	Park Royal	H41/27R	1960	
B3RA074	Grimsby-Cleethorpes (131)	NJV 993	Park Royal	H41/27R	1960	
B3RA075	Grimsby-Cleethorpes (132)	NJV 994	Park Royal	H41/27R	1960	
B3RA076	Grimsby-Cleethorpes (133)	NJV 995	Park Royal	H41/27R	1960	
2B3RA077	South Wales (1214)	XWN 161	Park Royal	H43/29F	1961	
2B3RA078	South Wales (1215)	YCY 795	Park Royal	H43/29F	1961	
2B3RA079	South Wales (1216)	YCY 796	Park Royal	H43/29F	1961	
2B3RA080	South Wales (1217)	YCY 797	Park Royal	H43/29F	1961	
2B3RA081	South Wales (1218)	YCY 798	Park Royal	H43/29F	1961	
2B3RA082	South Wales (1219)	YCY 799	Park Royal	H43/29F	1961	
2B3RA083	South Wales (1220)	YCY 800	Park Royal	H43/29F	1961	
2B3RA084	South Wales (1221)	YCY 801	Park Royal	H43/29F	1961	
B3RA085	East Yorkshire (700)	4700 AT	Park Royal	H45/28RD	1961	
B3RA086	East Yorkshire (701)	4701 AT	Park Royal	H45/28RD	1961	
B3RA087	East Yorkshire (702)	4702 AT	Park Royal	H45/28RD	1961	
B3RA088	East Yorkshire (703)	4703 AT	Park Royal	H45/28RD	1961	
B3RA089	East Yorkshire (704)	4704 AT	Park Royal	H45/28RD	1961	
B3RA090	East Yorkshire (705)	4705 AT	Park Royal	H45/28RD	1961	
B3RA091	East Yorkshire (706)	4706 AT	Park Royal	H45/28RD	1961	
B3RA092	East Yorkshire (707)	4707 AT	Park Royal	H45/28RD	1961	
B3RA093	East Yorkshire (708)	4708 AT	Park Royal	H45/28RD	1961	
B3RA094	East Yorkshire (709)	4709 AT	Park Royal	H45/28RD	1961	
B3RA095	East Yorkshire (710)	4710 AT	Park Royal	H45/28RD	1961	
B3RA096	East Yorkshire (711)	4711 AT	Park Royal	H45/28RD	1961	
B3RA097	East Yorkshire (712)	4712 AT	Park Royal	H45/28RD	1961	
B3RA098	East Yorkshire (713)	4713 AT	Park Royal	H45/28RD	1961	
B3RA099	East Yorkshire (714)	4714 AT	Park Royal	H45/28RD	1961	
B3RA100	East Yorkshire (715)	4715 AT	Park Royal	H45/28RD	1961	
2B3RA101	Rotherham (137)	VET 137	Park Royal	H43/27F	1961	
2B3RA102	Rotherham (138)	VET 138	Park Royal	H43/27F	1961	
2B3RA103	Rotherham (139)	VET 139	Park Royal	H43/27F	1961	
2B3RA104	Sheffield (525)	1925 WA	Park Royal	H43/29F	1961	
105	(not built)					
2B3RA106	East Yorkshire (716)	9716 AT	Park Royal	H43/29F	1962	
2B3RA107	East Yorkshire (717)	9717 AT	Park Royal	H43/29F	1962	
2B3RA108	East Yorkshire (718)	9718 AT	Park Royal	H43/29F	1962	
2B3RA109	East Yorkshire (719)	9719 AT	Park Royal	H43/29F	1962	
2B3RA110	East Yorkshire (720)	9720 AT	Park Royal	H43/29F	1962	
2B3RA111	East Yorkshire (721)	9721 AT	Park Royal	H43/29F	1962	
2B3RA112	East Yorkshire (722)	9722 AT	Park Royal	H43/29F	1962	
2B3RA113	East Yorkshire (723)	9723 AT	Park Royal	H43/29F	1962	
2B3RA114	East Yorkshire (724)	9724 AT	Park Royal	H43/29F	1962	
2B3RA115	East Yorkshire (725)	9725 AT	Park Royal	H43/29F	1962	
2B3RA116	East Yorkshire (726)	9726 AT	Park Royal	H43/29F	1962	
2B3RA117	East Yorkshire (727)	9727 AT	Park Royal	H43/29F	1962	
2B3RA118	East Yorkshire (728)	9728 AT	Park Royal	H43/29F	1962	
2B3RA119	East Yorkshire (729)	9729 AT	Park Royal	H43/29F	1962	
2B3RA120	East Yorkshire (730)	9730 AT	Park Royal	H43/29F	1962	
2B3RA121	City of Oxford (306)	306 MFC	Park Royal	H43/29F	1961	
2B3RA122	City of Oxford (307)	307 MFC	Park Royal	H43/29F	1961	
2B3RA123	City of Oxford (308)	308 MFC	Park Royal	H43/29F	1961	
2B3RA124	City of Oxford (309)	309 MFC	Park Royal	H43/29F	1961	
2B3RA125	City of Oxford (310)	310 MFC	Park Royal	H43/29F	1961	
2B3RA126	City of Oxford (311)	311 MFC	Park Royal	H43/29F	1961	
2B3RA127	City of Oxford (312)	312 MFC	Park Royal	H43/29F	1961	
2B3RA128	City of Oxford (313)	313 MFC	Park Royal	H43/29F	1961	
2B3RA129	City of Oxford (314)	314 MFC	Park Royal	H43/29F	1961	
2B3RA130	City of Oxford (315)	315 MFC	Park Royal	H43/29F	1961	
B3RA131	King Alfred, Winchester	323 CAA	Park Royal	H45/29R	1961	
B3RA132	King Alfred, Winchester	324 CAA	Park Royal	H45/29R	1961	
2B3RA133	Rotherham (140)	YET 940	Park Royal	H43/27F	1961	
2B3RA134	Rotherham (141)	YET 941	Park Royal	H43/27F	1961	
B3RA135	Leicester (215)	215 AJF	Park Royal	H41/31R	1961	
B3RA136	Leicester (216)	216 AJF	Park Royal	H41/31R	1961	
B3RA137	Leicester (217)	217 AJF	Park Royal	H41/31R	1961	
B3RA138	Leicester (218)	218 AJF	Park Royal	H41/31R	1961	
B3RA139	Leicester (219)	219 AJF	Park Royal	H41/31R	1961	

Chassis number	First owner	Registration	Body	Layout	New	Notes
2B3RA140	Baxter, Airdrie (78)	78 BVD	Park Royal	H43/29F	1961	
B3RA141	Red Rover, Aylesbury (7)	27 WKX	Park Royal	H45/31RD	1962	
2B3RA142	Smith, Barrhead	29 EGD	Park Royal	H43/29F	1961	
2B3RA143	Smith, Barrhead	30 EGD	Park Royal	H43/29F	1961	
2B3RA144	East Kent	YJG 807	Park Royal	H43/29F	1962	
2B3RA145	East Kent	YJG 808	Park Royal	H43/29F	1962	
2B3RA146	East Kent	YJG 809	Park Royal	H43/29F	1962	
2B3RA147	City of Oxford (316)	316 NJO	Park Royal	H40/25F	1962	
2B3RA148	City of Oxford (317)	317 NJO	Park Royal	H40/25F	1962	
2B3RA149	City of Oxford (318)	318 NJO	Park Royal	H40/25F	1963	
2B3RA150	City of Oxford (319)	319 NJO	Park Royal	H40/25F	1963	
2B3RA151	City of Oxford (320)	320 NJO	Park Royal	H40/25F	1963	
2B3RA152	City of Oxford (321)	321 NJO	Park Royal	H40/25F	1963	
2B3RA153	City of Oxford (322)	322 NJO	Park Royal	H40/25F	1963	
2B3RA154	City of Oxford (323)	323 NJO	Park Royal	H40/25F	1963	
2B3RA155	City of Oxford (324)	324 NJO	Park Royal	H40/25F	1963	
2B3RA156	City of Oxford (325)	325 NJO	Park Royal	H40/25F	1963	
2B3RA157	City of Oxford (326)	326 NJO	Park Royal	H40/25F	1963	
2B3RA158	City of Oxford (327)	327 NJO	Park Royal	H40/25F	1963	
2B3RA159	City of Oxford (328)	328 NJO	Park Royal	H40/25F	1963	
2B3RA160	Red Rover, Aylesbury (3)	6116 BH	Park Royal	H43/29F	1963	7
2B3RA161	Scottish Omnibuses (BB962)	9962 SF	Park Royal	H41/29F	1963	7
B3RA162	Leicester (220)	220 DRY	Park Royal	H45/31R	1962	
B3RA163	Leicester (221)	221 DRY	Park Royal	H45/31R	1962	
B3RA164	Leicester (222)	222 DRY	Park Royal	H45/31R	1962	
B3RA165	Lincoln (92)	TFE 535	Park Royal	H45/31R	1962	
B3RA166	Lincoln (93)	TFE 536	Park Royal	H45/31R	1962	
B3RA167	Lincoln (94)	TFE 537	Park Royal	H45/31R	1962	
B3RA168	Lincoln (95)	TFE 538	Park Royal	H45/31R	1962	
2B3RA169	East Yorkshire (742)	3742 RH	Park Royal	H43/29F	1963	
2B3RA170	East Yorkshire (743)	3743 RH	Park Royal	H43/29F	1963	
2B3RA171	East Yorkshire (744)	3744 RH	Park Royal	H43/29F	1963	
2B3RA172	East Yorkshire (745)	3745 RH	Park Royal	H43/29F	1963	
2B3RA173	East Yorkshire (746)	3746 RH	Park Royal	H43/29F	1963	
2B3RA174	East Yorkshire (747)	3747 RH	Park Royal	H43/29F	1963	
2B3RA175	East Yorkshire (748)	3748 RH	Park Royal	H43/29F	1963	
2B3RA176	East Yorkshire (749)	3749 RH	Park Royal	H43/29F	1963	
2B3RA177	East Yorkshire (750)	3750 RH	Park Royal	H43/29F	1963	
2B3RA178	East Yorkshire (751)	3751 RH	Park Royal	H43/29F	1963	
2B3RA179	East Yorkshire (752)	3752 RH	Park Royal	H43/29F	1963	
2B3RA180	East Yorkshire (753)	3753 RH	Park Royal	H43/29F	1963	
2B3RA181	East Yorkshire (754)	3754 RH	Park Royal	H43/29F	1963	
2B3RA182	East Yorkshire (755)	3755 RH	Park Royal	H43/29F	1963	
2B3RA183	East Yorkshire (756)	3756 RH	Park Royal	H43/29F	1963	

AEC Renown

Chassis number	First owner	Registration	Body	Layout	New	Notes
U204544	AEC (demonstrator)	7552 MX	Park Royal	H39/32F	1962	8
U204545	AEC (demonstrator)	8071 ML	Park Royal	H44/31F	1962	9
3B3RA001	South Wales (1254)	534 FCY	Willowbrook	H39/32F	1963	
3B3RA002	South Wales (1255)	535 FCY	Willowbrook	H39/32F	1963	
3B3RA003	South Wales (1256)	536 FCY	Willowbrook	H39/32F	1963	
3B3RA004	South Wales (1257)	537 FCY	Willowbrook	H39/32F	1963	
3B3RA005	South Wales (1258)	538 FCY	Willowbrook	H39/32F	1963	
3B3RA006	South Wales (1240)	303 ECY	Park Royal	H39/32F	1963	
3B3RA007	South Wales (1241)	304 ECY	Park Royal	H39/32F	1963	
3B3RA008	South Wales (1242)	305 ECY	Park Royal	H39/32F	1963	
3B3RA009	South Wales (1243)	306 ECY	Park Royal	H39/32F	1963	
3B3RA010	South Wales (1244)	307 ECY	Park Royal	H39/32F	1963	
3B3RA011	South Wales (1245)	308 ECY	Park Royal	H39/32F	1963	
3B3RA012	South Wales (1246)	309 ECY	Park Royal	H39/32F	1963	
3B3RA013	South Wales (1247)	310 ECY	Park Royal	H39/32F	1963	
3B3RA014	South Wales (1248)	311 ECY	Park Royal	H39/32F	1963	
3B3RA015	South Wales (1249)	312 ECY	Park Royal	H39/32F	1963	
3B3RA016	South Wales (1250)	313 ECY	Park Royal	H39/32F	1963	
3B3RA017	South Wales (1251)	314 ECY	Park Royal	H39/32F	1963	
3B3RA018	South Wales (1252)	314 ECY	Park Royal	H39/32F	1963	
3B3RA019	South Wales (1253)	316 ECY	Park Royal	H39/32F	1963	
3B3RA020	Leigh (25)	1972 TJ	East Lancs	H41/31R	1963	
3B3RA021	Leigh (26)	1973 TJ	East Lancs	H41/31R	1963	

Chassis number	First owner	Registration	Body	Layout	New	Notes
3B3RA022	Leigh (27)	1974 TJ	East Lancs	H41/31R	1963	
3B3RA023	Leigh (28)	1975 TJ	East Lancs	H41/31R	1963	
024	(not built)					
3B3RA025	Scottish Omnibuses (BB963)	9963 SF	Park Royal	H43/32F	1963	
3B3RA026	Smith, Barrhead	211 JUS	Park Royal	H43/32F	1963	
3B3RA027	Smith, Barrhead	212 JUS	Park Royal	H43/32F	1963	
028	(not built)					
3B3RA029	North Western (964)	VDB 964	Park Royal	H43/32F	1963	
3B3RA030	North Western (965)	VDB 965	Park Royal	H43/32F	1963	
3B3RA031	North Western (966)	VDB 966	Park Royal	H43/32F	1963	
3B3RA032	North Western (967)	VDB 967	Park Royal	H43/32F	1963	
3B3RA033	North Western (968)	VDB 968	Park Royal	H43/32F	1963	
3B3RA034	North Western (969)	VDB 969	Park Royal	H43/32F	1963	
3B3RA035	North Western (970)	VDB 970	Park Royal	H43/32F	1963	
3B3RA036	North Western (971)	VDB 971	Park Royal	H43/32F	1963	
3B3RA037	North Western (972)	VDB 972	Park Royal	H43/32F	1963	
3B3RA038	North Western (973)	VDB 973	Park Royal	H43/32F	1963	
3B3RA039	North Western (974)	VDB 974	Park Royal	H43/32F	1963	
3B3RA040	North Western (975)	VDB 975	Park Royal	H43/32F	1963	
3B3RA041	North Western (976)	VDB 976	Park Royal	H43/32F	1963	
3B3RA042	North Western (977)	VDB 977	Park Royal	H43/32F	1963	
3B3RA043	North Western (978)	VDB 978	Park Royal	H43/32F	1963	
3B3RA044	North Western (979)	VDB 979	Park Royal	H43/32F	1963	
3B3RA045	North Western (980)	VDB 980	Park Royal	H43/32F	1963	
3B3RA046	North Western (981)	VDB 981	Park Royal	H43/32F	1963	
3B3RA047	City of Oxford (329)	329 RJO	Park Royal	H38/27F	1963	
3B3RA048	City of Oxford (330)	330 RJO	Park Royal	H38/27F	1963	
3B3RA049	City of Oxford (331)	331 RJO	Park Royal	H38/27F	1963	
3B3RA050	City of Oxford (332)	332 RJO	Park Royal	H38/27F	1963	
3B3RA051	City of Oxford (333)	333 RJO	Park Royal	H38/27F	1963	
3B3RA052	City of Oxford (334)	334 RJO	Park Royal	H38/27F	1963	
3B3RA053	City of Oxford (335)	335 RJO	Park Royal	H38/27F	1963	
3B3RA054	City of Oxford (336)	336 RJO	Park Royal	H38/27F	1963	
3B3RA055	City of Oxford (337)	337 RJO	Park Royal	H38/27F	1963	
3B3RA056	City of Oxford (338)	338 RJO	Park Royal	H38/27F	1963	
3B3RA057	West Wales (47)	700 DTH	Willowbrook	H39/32F	1963	
3B3RA058	East Yorkshire (757)	9757 RH	Park Royal	H42/32F	1964	
3B3RA059	East Yorkshire (758)	9758 RH	Park Royal	H42/32F	1964	
3B3RA060	East Yorkshire (759)	9759 RH	Park Royal	H42/32F	1964	
3B3RA061	East Yorkshire (760)	9760 RH	Park Royal	H42/32F	1964	
3B3RA062	East Yorkshire (761)	9761 RH	Park Royal	H42/32F	1964	
3B3RA063	East Yorkshire (762)	9762 RH	Park Royal	H42/32F	1964	
3B3RA064	East Yorkshire (763)	9763 RH	Park Royal	H42/32F	1964	
3B3RA065	East Yorkshire (764)	9764 RH	Park Royal	H42/32F	1964	
3B3RA066	East Yorkshire (765)	9765 RH	Park Royal	H42/32F	1964	
3B3RA067	East Yorkshire (766)	9766 RH	Park Royal	H42/32F	1964	
3B3RA068	Western Welsh (713)	BKG 713B	Northern Counties	H38/29F	1964	
3B3RA069	Western Welsh (714)	BKG 714C	Northern Counties	H38/29F	1965	
3B3RA070	Western Welsh (715)	BKG 715C	Northern Counties	H38/29F	1965	
3B3RA071	Western Welsh (716)	BKG 716C	Northern Counties	H38/29F	1965	
3B3RA072	Western Welsh (717)	BKG 717C	Northern Counties	H38/29F	1965	
3B3RA073	Western Welsh (718)	BKG 718C	Northern Counties	H38/29F	1965	
3B3RA074	Western Welsh (719)	BKG 719C	Northern Counties	H38/29F	1965	
3B3RA075	Western Welsh (720)	BKG 720C	Northern Counties	H38/29F	1965	
3B3RA076	Western Welsh (721)	BKG 721C	Northern Counties	H38/29F	1965	
3B3RA077	Western Welsh (722)	BKG 722C	Northern Counties	H38/29F	1965	
3B3RA078	Western Welsh (723)	BKG 723C	Northern Counties	H38/29F	1965	
3B3RA079	Western Welsh (724)	BKG 724C	Northern Counties	H38/29F	1965	
3B3RA080	Western Welsh (725)	BKG 725C	Northern Counties	H38/29F	1965	
3B3RA081	Western Welsh (726)	BKG 726C	Northern Counties	H38/29F	1965	
3B3RA082	Western Welsh (727)	BKG 727C	Northern Counties	H38/29F	1965	
3B2RA083	King Alfred, Winchester	595 LCG	Park Royal	H44/31F	1964	
3B2RA084	King Alfred, Winchester	596 LCG	Park Royal	H44/31F	1964	
3B3RA085	City of Oxford (339)	339 TJO	Park Royal	H38/27F	1964	
3B3RA086	City of Oxford (340)	340 TJO	Park Royal	H38/27F	1964	
3B3RA087	City of Oxford (341)	341 TJO	Park Royal	H38/27F	1964	
3B3RA088	City of Oxford (342)	342 TJO	Park Royal	H38/27F	1964	
3B3RA089	City of Oxford (343)	343 TJO	Park Royal	H38/27F	1964	
3B3RA090	City of Oxford (344)	344 TJO	Park Royal	H38/27F	1964	
3B3RA091	City of Oxford (345)	345 TJO	Park Royal	H38/27F	1964	
3B3RA092	City of Oxford (346)	346 TJO	Park Royal	H38/27F	1964	
3B3RA093	City of Oxford (347)	347 TJO	Park Royal	H38/27F	1964	
094	(not built)					

Chassis number	First owner	Registration	Body	Layout	New	Notes
FDW75836	West Riding (1016)	BHL 367C	Roe	H43/32F	1965	
FDW75842	West Riding (1017)	BHL 368C	Roe	H43/32F	1965	
FDW75855	West Riding (1018)	BHL 369C	Roe	H43/32F	1965	
FDW75856	West Riding (1019)	BHL 370C	Roe	H43/32F	1965	
FDW75882	West Riding (1020)	BHL 371C	Roe	H43/32F	1965	
FDW75883	West Riding (1021)	BHL 372C	Roe	H43/32F	1965	
FDW75898	West Riding (1022)	BHL 373C	Roe	H43/32F	1965	
FDW75899	West Riding (1023)	BHL 374C	Roe	H43/32F	1965	
FDW75928	West Riding (1024)	BHL 375C	Roe	H43/32F	1965	
FDW75929	West Riding (1025)	BHL 376C	Roe	H43/32F	1965	
FDW75948	West Riding (1026)	BHL 377C	Roe	H43/32F	1965	
FDW75949	West Riding (1027)	BHL 378C	Roe	H43/32F	1965	
FDW75967	West Riding (1028)	BHL 379C	Roe	H43/32F	1965	
FDW75968	West Riding (1029)	BHL 380C	Roe	H43/32F	1965	

Notes

1	Sold to Birmingham Corporation (3228), 1957
2	Sold to South Wales Transport (1213), 1960
3	Sold to Barton Transport (805), 1958
4	Sold to Liverpool Corporation (E3), 1959
5	Sold to Osborne, Tollesbury (7), 1960
6	Sold to Osborne, Tollesbury (11), 1961
7	Ordered by Baxter, Airdrie
8	Sold to Burwell & District, 1965
9	Sold to Osborne, Tollesbury (18), 1963
10	Sold to Bamber Bridge Motor Services
11	Chassis originally supplied to Edinburgh Corporation
12	Built for China Motor Bus but not delivered. Registered 1964. Sold to Warner, Tewkesbury, 1966
13	Sold to West Riding for spares

Shining Brass

Book 1, Grades 1–3

Piano Accompaniment E♭

For use with

E♭ Soprano Cornet · E♭ Horn · E♭ Bass · E♭ Tuba

Composers

Tom Davoren, John Frith, Timothy Jackson, Peter Meechan,
Lucy Pankhurst, Philip Sparke and David A. Stowell

Project consultant

Nicky Daw

ABRSM

First published in 2012 by ABRSM (Publishing) Ltd, a wholly owned subsidiary of ABRSM

Reprinted in 2014, 2015, 2017, 2018

© 2012 by The Associated Board of the Royal Schools of Music
ISBN 978 1 84849 443 5
AB 3697

A CIP catalogue for this book is available from The British Library.

Cover design by www.adamhaystudio.com
Music origination by Andrew Jones
Printed in England by Caligraving Ltd, Thetford, Norfolk, on materials from sustainable sources

With particular thanks to Alan Bullard for his contribution to this project.

Contents

(Pianists should note that the solo line printed above the accompaniment reproduces the 𝄞 Brass part.)

A Knight's Tale

Philip Sparke

Romanza

Tom Davoren

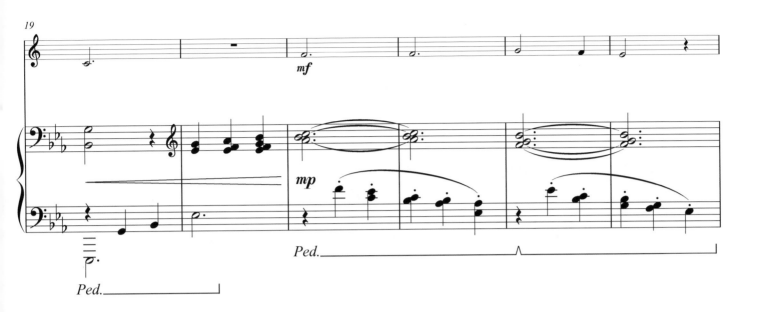

8

Strollin'

David A. Stowell

The lower octave may be omitted throughout.

in memory of Esbjörn Svensson

Waltz for E.

Tom Davoren

A Walk in the Rain

David A. Stowell

My Lady's Pavan

Philip Sparke

for Monti, the Beagle

Hangin' with Monti

Tom Davoren

Tennessee Rag

Philip Sparke

Rondo Olympia

Tom Davoren

Blank page

Sicilienne

Lucy Pankhurst

Broken Dreams

John Frith

27

Purple Shade

Peter Meechan

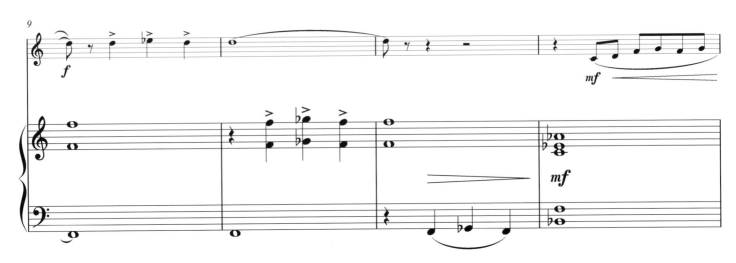